Wildlife of the deserts

The W⊕RLD of SURVIVAL
WILDLIFE
of the deserts
John Cloudsley-Thompson

HAMLYN
London · New York · Sydney · Toronto

Acknowledgements

Photographs

Ardea – Ian Beames 31 bottom, 32 bottom, 33 right, 67, 70 bottom; Ardea – Gert Behrens back jacket; Ardea – Hans and Judy Beste 53 top, 59 top; Ardea – Donald D. Burgess 46, 71 right; Ardea – Elizabeth S. Burgess 30 top; Ardea – M. D. England 46 top; Ardea – Kenneth W. Fink 10 top left, 13 top, 16 top, 54 top, 58 top, 66-67 top, 74, 93 bottom; Ardea – Clem Haagner 6, 23 top, 27 bottom right, 47 top, 47 bottom left, 52 top left, 52 bottom, 57 top; Ardea – Eric Lindgren 35 top right; Ardea – John Mason 37 bottom, 70 top left; Ardea – Pat Morris 36 bottom, 41, 60 bottom; Ardea – S. Roberts 10 top right; Ardea – Peter Steyn 35 top left, 47 bottom right; Ardea – Richard Waller 58 bottom; Ardea – Alan Weaving 25 bottom, 35 bottom left; Ardea – Wardene Weisser 45 bottom, 53 bottom, 54 bottom; Ardea – Tom Willock 8; J. Allan Cash, London 14 bottom, 20-21, 80 top, 88-89, 89; Bruce Coleman – Jen and Des Bartlett 23 bottom, 84 bottom; Bruce Coleman – Chris Bonington 84-85, 86 top; Bruce Coleman – Jane Burton 10 top centre, 25 top, 26 bottom, 28 top, 35 bottom right, 37 top, 38-39, 55 top, 63; Bruce Coleman – Bob and Clara Calhoun 25 top; Bruce Coleman – J. A. L. Cooke 31 top, 32 top; Bruce Coleman – Eric Crichton front jacket; Bruce Coleman – Gerald Cubitt 77, 78; Bruce Coleman – Stephen Dalton 34; Bruce Coleman – L. R. Dawson 57 bottom; Bruce Coleman – Nicholas Devore 85 bottom, 86 bottom; Bruce Coleman – Francisco Erize 61 top; Bruce Coleman – M. P. L. Fogden endpapers, 12, 28 bottom right; Bruce Coleman – James Hancock 11 top; Bruce Coleman – David Hughes 78-79; Bruce Coleman – Jade Photographics 94 top; Bruce Coleman – M. Timothy O'Keefe 93 top; Bruce Coleman – Charlie Ott 26 top, 27 top, 62-63; Bruce Coleman – Douglas Pike 94 bottom; Bruce Coleman – Prato 81; Bruce Coleman – W. E. Ruth 9; Bruce Coleman – John Shaw 36 top; Bruce Coleman – James Simon title page, 45 top right; Bruce Coleman – Stouffer Productions 61 bottom; Bruce Coleman – Norman Owen Tomalin 7; Robert Harding Associates, London 66-67 bottom, 90; Robert Harding Associates – Jon Gardey 21 bottom, 27 bottom left, 79 bottom, 87; Robert Harding Associates – F. Jackson 80 left; Robert Harding Associates – Walter Rawlings 17 top, 82 top; Robert Harding Associates – John Stathatos 82 bottom; Frank W. Lane – A. Christiansen 51 bottom; Frank W. Lane – E. J. Davis 51 top; Frank W. Lane – Mrs J. E. H. Finch 22 top; Oxford Scientific Films 21 top, 42 bottom, 70 top right, 75 bottom; Oxford Scientific Films – J. A. L. Cooke 30 bottom, 75 top; Survival Anglia Ltd 82-83; Survival Anglia Ltd – Jen and Des Bartlett 22 bottom, 24 top, 29, 38, 40-41, 45 top left, 48 left, 48 right, 48-49, 52 top right, 59 bottom, 60 top, 64, 65, 72, 72-73; Survival Anglia Ltd – Joel Bennett 66 top; Survival Anglia Ltd – Rod Borland 14 top, 18-19, 28 bottom left, 33 left, 44, 50, 92; Survival Anglia Ltd – Cindy Buxton 43 bottom; Survival Anglia Ltd – Lee Lyon 10 bottom, 55 bottom, 76-77; Survival Anglia Ltd – Dieter and Mary Plage 11 bottom, 24 bottom, 43 top; Survival Anglia Ltd – David de Vries 66 left; Survival Anglia Ltd – Colin Willock 13 bottom, 42 top, 49 top, 49 inset, 68, 69 bottom, 69 top; ZEFA – A. Foley 91.

Illustrations

Creative Cartography Ltd., and Ray and Corinne Burrows.

Published 1979 by
The Hamlyn Publishing Group Limited
London · New York · Sydney · Toronto
Astronaut House, Feltham, Middlesex, England
Text © Copyright The Hamlyn Publishing Group Limited 1979
Illustrations © Copyright The Hamlyn Publishing Group Limited 1979
WORLD OF SURVIVAL
Registered Trademark

ISBN 0 600 39451 4

Printed in Italy

Contents

Desert survival

A desert is a harsh, wild, but exciting place in which to live. It is not easy for plants and animals to survive there because all living things need water – and that is just what you do not find much of in a desert! So they have to make do with very little, or almost none at all, and what makes matters worse, many desert regions get dreadfully hot in the daytime. Now, when we humans get hot, we sweat and our bodies are cooled as our sweat evaporates. Soon we begin to feel thirsty and have to take a long drink to replenish the liquid we have lost. But, in the desert, there is usually no water, and we would very quickly become desiccated and die if we could not drink. Unlike us, many plants and animals are adapted to survive long periods of heat and drought, and it is mainly these adaptations that we will be thinking about in this book.

How to survive in a hot climate

There are several different ways by which animals are able to survive in hot deserts. Small forms, like scorpions, jerboas and kangaroo rats make deep burrows in which they hide from the midday heat, only coming out at night when the air is cooler and more damp. Birds cannot dig holes for themselves, of course. Some, like owls and

Left:
The camel, 'ship of the desert', is wonderfully adapted for life in arid environments. The dromedary, seen here in the Kalahari, originally came from the Middle East but has been introduced by Man as a beast of burden into many other desert regions.

Below:
The Polar Bear, largest carnivore of Arctic regions, survives mainly on seals and fishes.

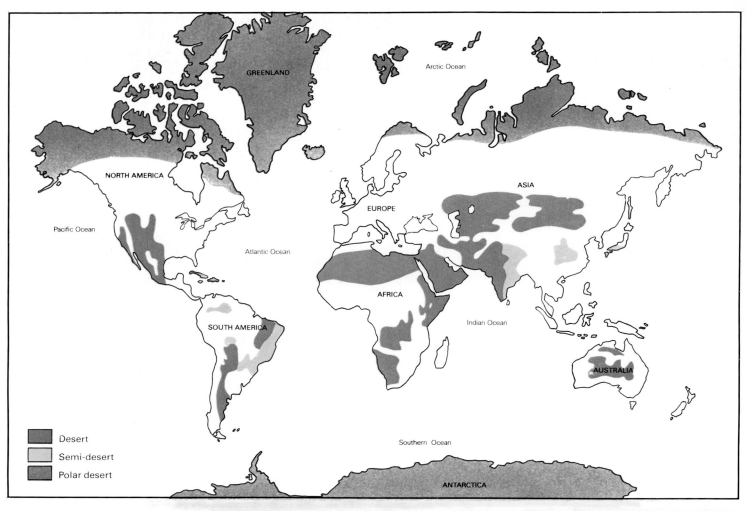

Above:
The principal desert regions of the world.
The tropical deserts of South America, Africa and Australia have hot summers and warm winters; the sub-tropical deserts of North America and Asia have hot summers and cool winters; while the polar deserts of the Arctic and Antarctic have cold summers and very cold winters.

Right:
Wapiti (*Cervus canadensis*) in a snowstorm. Herds of this large deer are found in North America, Central and North-East Asia, in temperate, cold, and dry habitats.

Desert
Semi-desert
Polar desert

GREENLAND
Arctic Ocean
NORTH AMERICA
ASIA
Pacific Ocean
EUROPE
Atlantic Ocean
AFRICA
SOUTH AMERICA
Indian Ocean
AUSTRALIA
Southern Ocean
ANTARCTICA

nightjars feed at night and hide away during the day down holes in trees and cacti, or in cracks in rocks. Larger birds, such as eagles, vultures and kites pass the day soaring high in the sky where the air is cooler. Small birds have the greatest difficulty of all. When it is very hot they can only hide in the shade of rocks and bushes, but even so, they may have to pant in order to keep cool. Most small birds are found near oases, pools and rivers, for they need to drink frequently in order to replace the water lost by evaporation.

Camels, antelopes and other large mammals are somewhat better off. Although they cannot dig holes to hide in, their very size helps them to keep alive during the heat of the day. Their bodies take a long time to heat up so they do not need to sweat very much until the afternoon, and this saves precious water. Then, they have a very small surface area compared with their size. The larger an animal is, the more it can afford to lose moisture through its skin. This is because there is more water in the body for the same amount of surface when an animal is large like a camel, than when it is small, like a little bird.

How to survive in a cold climate

In polar deserts, on the other hand, the problem is mainly one of keeping warm rather than cool. Small animals, like the

Snowshoe Rabbit (*Lepus americanus*), are able to tunnel under the snow in winter. Even there the cold is bitter, so they need to have dense fur. Large animals, such as elk and polar bears are helped by their size but they also need hair that is long and thick.

Survival of the fattest – and the thinnest

Mammals and birds which live in cold regions tend to be larger than their relatives which inhabit warmer places. Warm-blooded animals produce heat throughout their bodies, but especially in the liver, and lose it on the surface. Large animals, having a smaller surface in relation to their bulk than do smaller animals, are able to keep their heat in more efficiently. A good example of this relationship is provided by the bears. Largest of all the bears is the giant Kodiak Bear (*Ursus middendorffi*) of Kodiak Island in the Gulf of Alaska. The smallest is the Sun Bear (*Helarctos malayanus*), which lives in the warm tropics of south-eastern Asia. Large size is thus an adaptation to cold climate, while smaller size is an adaptation to warmer climates – as far as the regulation of body temperature is concerned. But, to economize on water in hot deserts, it is better for an animal to be larger. The actual size of an animal is therefore affected by these two opposing tendencies.

The relationship between climate and body size does not apply to cold-blooded

Above:
The Snowshoe Rabbit or Varying Hare, seen here in Alaska, tunnels under snow in winter. The pads of its hind legs are almost twice as long as those of an ordinary rabbit and help it to walk on soft snow without sinking in.

creatures such as reptiles. These animals have to gain heat through the surface of their bodies. They cannot keep warm in a cold climate if their bodies are too large. For this reason, large reptiles are to be found only in the warmer regions of the world.

The shape of an animal's body is also related to the climate. Animals that live in cold places tend to be stoutly built with short limbs and extremities. This cuts down the amount of surface area through which

heat is lost. The goats and camels of hot deserts have longer legs and a more lanky build than the ones which live in cooler regions. The foxes provide another good example. The Arctic Fox (*Alopex lagopus*) has a short snout and very small ears. The Common Red Fox (*Vulpes vulpes*) of northern temperate regions has a long snout and large ears, while the Kit Fox (*Vulpes velox*) and the Fennec Fox (*Fennecus zerda*), which live in hot deserts, are smaller and

more slender than the red fox, and have enormous ears. These big ears not only enable them to hear better, but also help to keep them cool.

Elephants, with their huge bodies, seem to contradict the rule, because they live in the tropics. But this is not really the case, because they have enormous ears which increase the surface area tremendously, and act as radiators to give off heat. This is especially true of the African Elephant (*Loxodonta africana*) – the Indian Elephant (*Elephas maximus*) keeps more to shady forests, and its ears are much smaller than those of its African cousin. Elephants keep their ears fanning backwards and forwards when it is very hot, and sometimes squirt water over themselves. They can survive in very hot dry places if they have enough to drink. They will even dig for water in the sand of dry river beds.

A similar kind of relationship also applies to human beings. Eskimos, living in the cold North, have a stocky build with short limbs and flat noses. Their physique contrasts markedly with the tall, long-legged Dinka and Zulu peoples of tropical Africa.

Top left:
The natives of tropical regions, such as this young Masai warrior in Kenya, tend to be tall with long legs. In contrast, the Eskimos of the Arctic have a stocky build.

Opposite bottom:
The enormous ears of the African Elephant increase its surface area and serve as radiators to give off excess heat.

Left:
The Indian or Asian Elephant, has much smaller ears than its African cousin, but lives in cooler places such as the shady forests of Sri Lanka.

Survival of the fittest

The largest desert in the world is the Great Palaearctic desert, which includes the Sahara and Somali deserts of northern Africa, the Arabian, Iranian and Turkestan deserts, the Indian or Thar desert and the Takla-Makan and Gobi deserts of central Asia. Next in size, and somewhat less arid, is the Australian desert, followed by the Great American desert – which includes the Mojave, Great Basin, Sonoran and Chihuahuan deserts of south-western North America. Much of Argentina is occupied by the Patagonian desert, while South Africa has the Namib and Kalahari deserts. The desert with the lowest rainfall of all, averaging under 25 millimetres (1 inch) of rain per year, is the Atacama of Peru and Chile. The polar deserts stretch over nearly as much of the earth as do tropical and subtropical deserts but, unlike them, the polar deserts are practically uninhabited.

The main problem facing plants and animals in all these deserts is shortage of water. Heat and cold are not so difficult to contend with. Nevertheless, scarcity of water, temperature extremes, strong winds and lack of shelter all influence the animals that live in desert regions, as we shall see in greater detail later on. A harsh fight for survival takes place in all the hot, dry and ice-bound regions of the world, and only the fittest plants and animals are able to survive in such places.

Opposite page:
The White Sands of New Mexico are formed of gypsum from a dried-up lake bed.

Above:
Beavertail and other cacti flourish in the deserts of south-western North America. Cacti have been introduced into deserts throughout the world.

Below:
Snow and ice cover most of the bleak Antarctic landscape. Seals, penguins and other animals depend mainly on fishes for nourishment.

Climate and soil

Although everyone knows what is meant by the word 'desert', and could describe what a desert looks like, it is still rather difficult to pinpoint exactly what it is that makes deserts quite as barren and unfriendly as they actually are. For example, you may say that deserts are hot. But deserts are not always hot – indeed, the winter can be very cold in the Gobi and Great Basin deserts, while the Arctic and Antarctic regions are the coldest places on earth. You may decide that deserts are always dry – but sometimes they experience very heavy rain storms and devastating floods. They are, however, usually dry for most of the year, and this is the important point. Again, there may be plenty of water in the desert wastes of the Arctic and Antarctic, but it is frozen into ice for most of the time and cannot be used by plants and animals, so it might just as well not be there! Lack of available water and the extreme cold, are what turn the polar regions into desert wastelands – very beautiful to look at but very difficult to live in. If we need to have a definition, it can only be that deserts are places thoroughly inhospitable to life.

Wastelands of the world

To an astronaut orbiting the world, nearly one-fifth of the land surface appears brown and lifeless – because there is not enough vegetation to make it green. These areas have warm or hot summers and relatively cool winters which, in some areas, such as Mongolia, may be really quite cold. Water is always in short supply, however, because throughout most of the year more is lost by evaporation than ever falls as rain. The brown desert wastelands occupy a sizeable portion of the earth's land mass, but this huge area is by no means fixed. During the last hundred years or so, the deserts have been expanding at an alarming rate. Regions south of the Sahara, in Somalia, and on the borders of the Thar desert of India and Pakistan, for instance, which were green and fertile within living memory, are now dry and barren. This is due almost entirely to unwise human activities – in particular, felling trees to provide fuel for cooking, and permitting overgrazing by cattle, sheep and goats. It is claimed that as much land has been changed into desert during the past century, as would suffice to provide food for the world's entire human population! To the astronaut the vast polar regions appear white with ice and snow. Here the summers are generally cool or cold, and the winters, bitterly cold.

The distribution of areas where there is little or no rain is due mainly to the way in which the atmosphere circulates around the world. Tropical and subtropical deserts are the result of more or less permanent belts of high pressure. When the barometer registers a high reading, we know that we are going to have a spell of fine weather. Dry air is more dense than moist air so that, when the needle of the barometer goes up, it means that the air is dry. When the air pressure is high during most of the year, and the sun blazes down from a cloudless sky, the earth becomes a scorched desert. This is what we find in the Sahara, in Arabia, and in the Great Indian desert, for example.

The deserts of central Asia are so far from the sea that the wind has lost nearly all its moisture by the time it gets to them so no rain falls. The same is true of much of the Sahara, the Australian outback, and the Great Basin deserts of North America. Such deserts are called 'interior continental deserts' because they are found in the interiors of continental masses.

Rain-shadow deserts are situated on the lee sides of mountain ranges, which cause the winds to rise and drop their moisture in the form of rain. For instance, the Mojave desert of California is dry in winter because the wind that might be expected to bring rain loses all its moisture while it is crossing the Sierra Nevada mountains, and is dry when it gets to the other side. Many deserts are caused by a combination of rain-shadow and distance from the sea.

The Namib of south-west Africa, the Atacama of Chile and Peru, and the coastal regions of Lower California are almost always rainless, although they are often drenched with chilly dew. These deserts are caused by the cool ocean currents that flow past the shore bringing fog but no rain. They never get very warm, however, and are known as 'cool coastal deserts'.

The effects of climate

The plants and animals that inhabit desert places are exposed to great climatic extremes. Very hot days may be followed by cool or cold nights. Long periods of drought are broken by torrential storms and flooding. Hot deserts, such as the Sahara and Kalahari, have no cold season, but, in cooler deserts, like the Great Basin and Gobi, one or more of the winter months may be so cold that its mean temperature is below 6 °C (43 °F)!

When the air is moist or there are clouds in the sky, the sun's heat cannot beat too fiercely on the ground during the day. On the other hand, at night, clouds act like blankets to keep the earth warm. In the desert, however, there is very little moisture to shade the ground during the day and few clouds to keep the land warm after

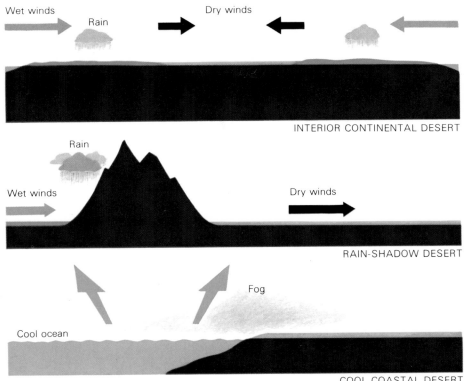

Wet winds
Rain
Dry winds
INTERIOR CONTINENTAL DESERT

Rain
Wet winds
Dry winds
RAIN-SHADOW DESERT

Fog
Cool ocean
COOL COASTAL DESERT

dark. That is why daytime temperatures are so high and why the nights are so cold.

The sun shines continuously during the summer in the Arctic and Antarctic, while throughout the winter – nearly six months of darkness – the bitter cold is unabated. There are no proper days or nights. Even during the long, cool summer, the snow and ice melt only for a few weeks so that the vegetation has very little time each year in which to grow. This is quite as big a handicap as having to make do with occasional scattered showers as plants in hot deserts have to do.

Although desert rainfall tends to be seasonal, it is most erratic. Some years can be quite wet while, in others, there is no rain at all. For example, Cairo had only 18 reasonably heavy showers between 1890 and 1919 and, in 17 years out of the 30, there was no rain at all. Then, on 17 January 1919, so much rain fell that the city was flooded. Boats from the Nile sailed in the streets, trams were sunk in the mud up to the level of their windows, and houses of unbaked bricks in the suburbs melted away like lumps of sugar.

I experienced an impressive example of desert rainfall when we were struck by a devastating thunderstorm one evening in northern Chad. We had almost finished setting up camp when the gale began. There was barely time to secure the primus cooker and rescue the pots and pans before the rain poured from the sky. Within minutes, the entire landscape, brilliantly lit by lightning, was inundated with water. Looking out from our vehicle, we seemed to be floating in a vast rippling sea although the water was not very deep. When the rain stopped as abruptly as it had begun, we literally had to shout at each other to be

Above:
Interior continental deserts are so far from the sea that the air has lost all its moisture before it reaches them. Rain-shadow deserts are in the lee of mountain ranges – on which rain falls so that the air becomes dry before reaching them. Cool coastal deserts are rainless because air masses descend over nearby cold ocean currents which produce chilly fog.

Opposite top:
Low-altitude deserts are mostly dry but *wadis*, such as the Kuiseb River of the Namib desert, become roaring torrents after a heavy rainstorm.

Opposite bottom:
Most desert wastelands are man-made or have been greatly enlarged by human misuse. These Karomojong ploughing with oxen in northern Uganda will not harm the environment if they leave the land fallow for several years after cultivating it.

15

Right:
The Ocotillo of the American deserts
is a dramatic sight during the rainy
season when leaves and crimson
blossoms adorn its branches. Most of
the year it is bare to conserve
moisture.

Opposite top:
The effect of wind erosion, caused by
dust particles in the air, created the
weird, statuesque appearance of these
rocks in Monument Valley, Arizona.

Opposite bottom:
Desert regions of the world.

heard above the fantastic chorus of croaking toads and stridulating insects. Next morning the water had disappeared. After crossing 80 kilometres (50 miles) of mud we reached dry sand.

In most desert regions, the presence of dry river beds, known generally by the Arabic name *wadi* shows that rain must fall occasionally. Most of it runs away very quickly, for there is little vegetation to check its flow, and the ground is so hard that water does not readily soak in. The actual amount of rain that falls does not matter very much to the desert plants and animals since most of it is wasted. More important is the length of time between the storms which produce enough water for seeds to germinate and grow.

Animals depend, directly or indirectly, upon plants for their food. Of course, some animals, like foxes and hyaenas, are carnivorous and feed upon the bodies of other animals. But the animals they eat either themselves eat plants or else feed on other animals which do. When there is only a short growing season each year, there can be very little vegetation, so the number of animals is greatly restricted. In tropical and subtropical deserts, the growing season is limited to the period immediately following rain storms. In polar deserts the growing season is also short. It takes place in summer when some of the ice melts and the surface of the ground thaws. Below a depth of a few centimetres the soil is permanently frozen. Because water is so scarce, there is not much vegetation. Consequently, shortage of food adds to shortage of water and extremes of heat and cold in making any desert a harsh environment for animal life.

Because the desert climate is so variable, average temperatures are of little importance as far as plants and animals are concerned. What matters are temperatures so high that they can kill, or temperatures so low that they cause frost damage. An annual range of shade temperatures from $-2°C$ (28°F) to $52.5°C$ (127°F) has been recorded from Wadi Halfa in the Sudan. This, of course, was before Wadi Halfa became submerged beneath the waters of Lake Nubia – held back by the High Dam at Aswan!

As well as lack of moisture in the form of rain, and extreme temperatures caused by the absence of clouds, the shortage of moisture in the air itself has a harmful effect upon plant and animal life. This is because during the day, water evaporates more readily from the leaves of plants and the bodies of animals in dry air than it does in humid air. This drying out makes the effects of drought and heat even more acute.

At night, on the other hand, when the temperature drops, the air becomes more humid. In some deserts it may become

NEARCTIC DESERT

GREAT AMERICAN DESERT

Mojave Desert

Sonoran Desert

Chihuahuan Desert

ATACAMA DESERT

so damp that dew falls. Then insects, snails and other small animals are able to drink. Even when there is no dew, dried leaves and other plant matter absorb moisture in the same way as blotting paper. Animals are sometimes able to extract this moisture by chewing the vegetable material.

The relentless winds

The desert is open country, so it is difficult to find shelter from the constant winds. These blow hardest during the day and their effect is enhanced by the drought, high temperature and lack of vegetation. In several desert regions the distribution of plants is determined mainly by the presence or absence of shelter from the wind. The wind blows harder in the Antarctic than anywhere else in the world.

Desert winds carry small particles of dust and sand which steadily wear away the desert rocks. This erosion sometimes produces weird and statuesque effects like those to be seen in southern Algeria and in Monument Valley, Arizona. Larger grains

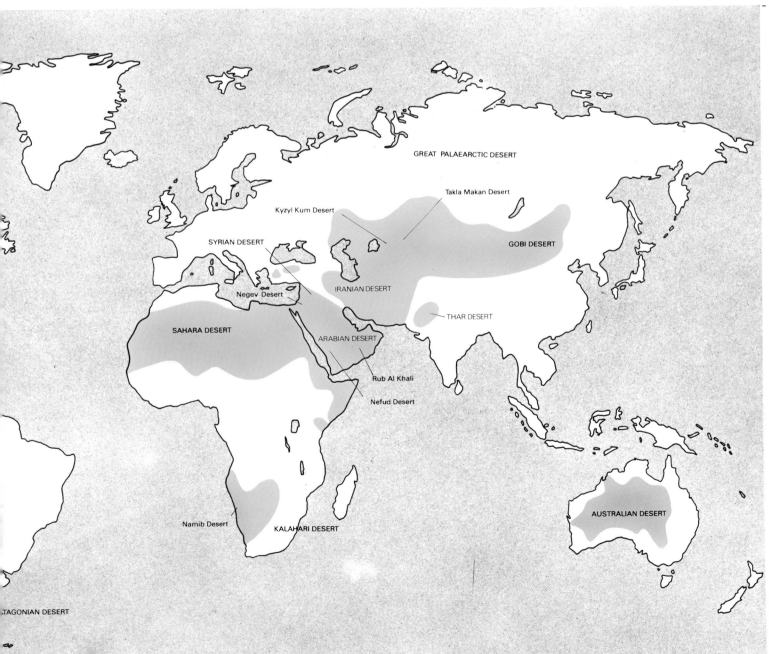

of sand are blown across the surface of the desert, to collect and form dunes. As a result of erosion, desert sand grains tend to become quite smooth and rounded. For this reason, unlike sand grains from the beach, they do not hurt much when they get into your eyes. It is worth remembering though, that if you should have to eat during a sand storm it will be less off-putting if you do not let your teeth meet while you are chewing!

A sandstorm can be so unpleasant that it is given special names in the different deserts of the world. It is *khamsin* in Egypt, *harmattan* in West Africa, *sirocco* in Arabia, *haboob* in the Sudan and *brickfielder* in Australia. I remember a sandstorm in Libya when the air was so thick that I could not even see a glimmer from a lighted torch at night at a distance of five paces. On another occasion, when my wife and I were driving across the Sahara, a sandstorm blew overhead. Although there was no dust at ground level, it became so dark that we had to switch on the headlights in order to see the ground.

Equally spectacular are the *chubaseos* or tropical hurricanes of the North American deserts, where wind speeds sometimes reach 150 kilometres (93 miles) per hour. Even on still days, whirlwinds or 'dust-devils' are a threat to small animals which are often sucked upwards, sometimes to a great height.

Adapting to desert conditions

The conditions which larger animals and human beings have to endure in the desert are quite different from those experienced by small animals. When a storm is blowing, scorpions and insects, lizards and jerboas take refuge in holes and crevices, under stones or down their burrows. The temperature, humidity and air movements in these small spaces together make up what is known as their 'microclimate'.

Microclimates are always less extreme than the macroclimate of the desert outside. The temperature in the burrow is lower than that outside during the day, and at night it is higher. The atmosphere is moister and the air almost completely still. By burrowing deeply or entering a cave or rock fissure, an animal can avoid the extreme heat and drought of the daytime and, by leaving the burrow at night it can even avoid the peak underground temperature, for there is often a considerable time-lag before heat begins to penetrate deeply into the sand.

Plants are at a disadvantage compared with animals for they cannot move into the shade. Grasses and other small plants, however, are able to evade the hottest weather by completing their life cycles during the short rainy season and passing the remainder of the year as fruits or seeds lying dormant in the soil. The only other alterna-

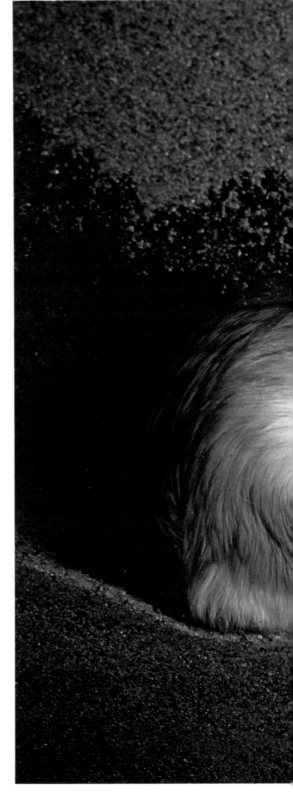

tive for plants is to develop resistance to drought, and the larger shrubs and trees of hot deserts are well adapted for this.

Polar regions look quite different from hot deserts but, as far as the vegetation is concerned, they have surprisingly much in common. The plants of polar deserts are small, close to the ground, and widely separated, with bare soil or rock between them. They are almost always perennial, however, because the growing season is not long enough for them to complete their life cycle at such low temperatures. Their leaves often have leathery, waxy or hairy surfaces which serve to reduce water-loss

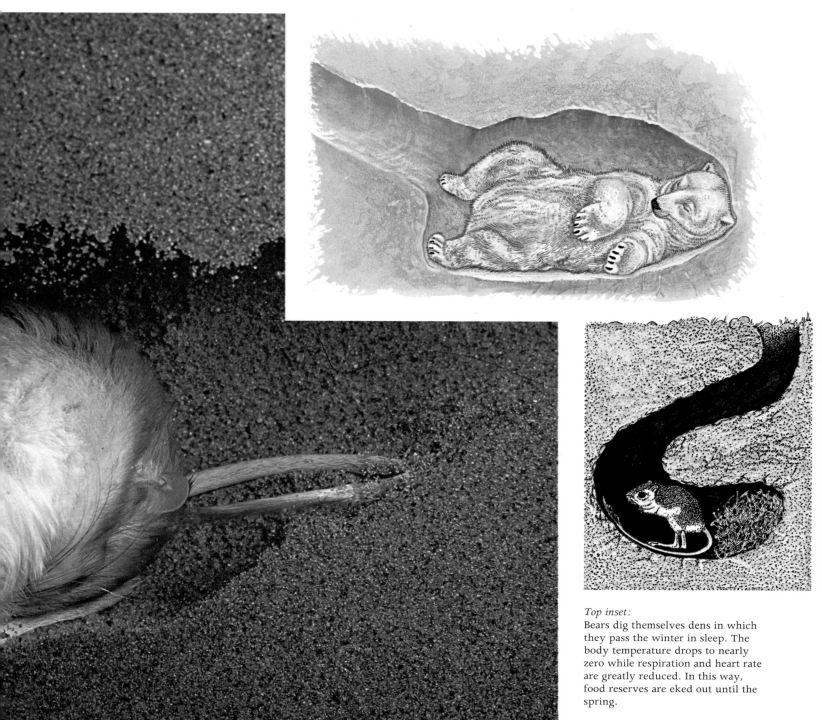

Top inset:
Bears dig themselves dens in which they pass the winter in sleep. The body temperature drops to nearly zero while respiration and heart rate are greatly reduced. In this way, food reserves are eked out until the spring.

Above:
Kangaroo-rats avoid the heat of the day by hiding in deep burrows when the microclimate is cool and comparatively moist. They come out at night to forage for the grass seeds and vegetable matter on which they feed.

Left:
The private life of this Namib desert Gerbil in captivity can be studied through the glass against which its burrow has been constructed.

by evaporation – like those of the drought-resistant plants of hot deserts.

The desert landscape

Plants need soil to grow in, and soil is produced by the wearing away and weathering of the rocks that make up the crust of the earth. Weathering can be mechanical, chemical or biological. In polar deserts, the rocks are worn and polished by the movement of ice and glaciers. In tropical and subtropical deserts, exposed rocks become very hot during the day and are cooled relatively quickly at night. This gives rise to continual expansion and contraction and

causes them to break up into smaller and smaller pieces. Rocks and stones are gradually eroded or worn away by sandstorms – another kind of mechanical weathering.

Surprisingly, chemical weathering – erosion of the rock by chemicals dissolved in rain water, is important in hot as well as in polar deserts. The explanation for this is that, although rainstorms are rare in deserts their effect is greatest where bare rocks and soil are unprotected by vegetation. Also, the chemicals in the water are more reactive at higher temperatures.

Very little biological weathering takes place in deserts. Biological weathering is

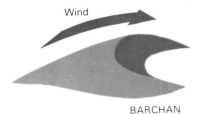

Wind

BARCHAN

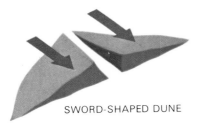

TRANSVERSE

SWORD-SHAPED DUNE

STAR-SHAPED DUNE

Above:
Desert sand dunes vary in form according to the strength and direction of the wind.

Above right:
The Landrover in the foreground indicates the size of these enormous sand dunes in the south of Libya.

Opposite top:
These moving crescent-shaped 'barchan' dunes are crossing the salty crust of a dried up lake or 'kavir' in north-eastern Iran.

Opposite bottom:
The steep slope on the lee side of a dune in the Algerian sand sea, or 'erg', near In Guezzam.

caused by earthworms and insects boring into the soil and breaking it up, and digesting fallen leaves and vegetation to form humus. Bacteria and other microbes help them. But, polar deserts are too cold for worms – which cannot live for long in frozen earth – while tropical and sub-tropical deserts are much too dry. Worms have moist skins so they dry up very quickly, and microbes and soil insects cannot stand prolonged drought. So there is little humus in desert soils to hold such moisture as is available – another reason why plants do not grow well unless they are watered or irrigated.

Rain also causes erosion, and temporary water-courses or *wadis* are common in desert regions. In America they are called *arroyos* and, in the Sudan, *khors*. Dry throughout most of the year, and sometimes for several years, they become roaring torrents after a single shower. Sand is scoured from their banks and soil from the ground is washed out to form immense flat plains. When these plains are covered with a mosaic of gravel, they are known as *reg*.

When all the sand has been removed by wind and rain to leave bare rocks polished by the wind, the desert is known as *hammada*. Areas in which sand and dust have been deposited often take the form of *ergs* – vast, sandy wastes occupied by great masses of dunes.

Desert sand dunes may grow to an enormous size, reaching a height of 200 metres (660 feet) or more, in the central Sahara and the Empty Quarter of Arabia. You can see them, row upon row, as your aeroplane flies high above the desert. Some of them are believed to have existed for many thousands of years.

Most sand dunes are horizontal, or shaped like a sword with a long blade and a short, bent handle. They are caused by winds blowing constantly from the same direction and leaving deep troughs. When the winds blow from different directions, the dunes they form are star-shaped. The

most interesting dunes, and the ones that move most quickly are crescent-shaped, like a new moon. They are found where sand is relatively scarce and where the wind direction is constant. They are called *barchans* and move with their horns in front, pointing forward. This is because sand is blown more quickly over the advancing points than over the central hump of the dune.

Most desert and near-desert regions support some degree of vegetation, despite their dry climates. The least amount of plant life is to be found in areas of hammada (stony desert) and clay.

Sandy desert usually has a greater variety of plants, except on moving dunes where plants do not get a chance to become established. Wherever the plants do best, there you will find the most animals. However, animals can even live in completely barren desert, feeding on dry grass and dead leaves blown there from more productive places.

The coming of rain

Above:
Brought to life by a shower some months earlier, these desert flowers are blooming on a red sand hill near Ayers Rock in Central Australia.

Right:
Cactus flowers are often extremely beautiful. This photograph shows the bloom of a Rainbow Cactus in Arizona.

Plant life is controlled both by rainfall and by soil. The type of soil depends upon the parent rock from which it has been weathered, so even deserts with the same sort of climate, may have very different kinds of vegetation. However, every desert's floral season is a short one. Within a few days of rain, the sand becomes green with sprouting grasses and other small plants whose entire life cycles are compressed into a few weeks. During this time, the seeds have to grow into plants which flower and produce more seeds, before the ground dries up again and the plants wither away. Plants which only grow at the time of the rain, and pass the dry season in the form of resistant seeds, are usually called 'ephemerals'.

Plants of hot deserts
In the deserts of North America particularly, the short growing season provides a show of wild beauty. The desert is strewn with clumps of brilliant colour. White daisies, yellow eriophyllum and purple nama blossoms spring from the inhospitable sand, while cacti are garlanded with dazzling flowers. In the hills of Tunisia too, beyond the eucalyptus trees of Zaghouan, from where the Romans brought their water along stone aquaducts to Carthage, the ground in spring is set with blue convolvulus, yellow dandelions and red vetch, producing quite an alpine effect in the bright sunshine. The Kalahari desert blossoms after rain, but large areas of the Great Palaearctic and Australian deserts produce only grasses.

In the Mojave and Colorado deserts of south-western North America, there are normally two rainy seasons during the year – in summer and in winter – each of which produces its own crop of plants. The summer annuals sprout after the summer rains and complete their life cycles rapidly. The seeds that they produce do not germinate when the winter rains fall, but remain dormant in the soil until the following summer. The plants whose seeds germinate after the winter rains, flower in the spring and are quite different from summer annuals. Only a few species blossom at all times of the year.

Experiments have shown that, when soil from this desert area is kept at various temperatures and then watered, the seeds of summer annuals will only germinate above about 20°C (68°F) while those of winter annuals sprout below this temperature. The seeds of grasses from the Sahara will not grow, even when moistened, until they have experienced the hot, dry summer.

Two kinds of annual plants are found in the Negev desert of Israel, where most of the rain falls in winter. Some plants are winter annuals which complete their life cycles during the wet season. A smaller group of summer annuals includes plants that continue to grow throughout the hot, dry summer, and produce mature seeds in the autumn. Some plants produce seeds impregnated with salt which prevents germination from taking place until it has been washed away by rain. Other plants have seeds of two kinds, flat and humped, which require varying amounts of water before they will germinate.

Many ephemeral, drought-evading plants produce seeds which have special features to aid their dispersal. Some seeds have barbs and spines which hook onto the hairs of passing animals. The legs of goats are sometimes completely covered with the spikelets of bur grass. These spikelets do not fall off for a long time so there is a good chance of the seeds being carried to places that are suitable for germination and growth.

Large numbers of the seeds of certain desert grasses become entwined to form dense, round balls which are blown along by the wind. As the sharp points of the seeds come in contact with the ground, they become anchored and pull away from the ball, which eventually disintegrates. Afterwards, changes in the humidity of the air cause the seeds to twist, so that they drill their way into the soil, where they stay until rain falls and they are able to germinate.

The fruits of some desert plants are also blown about for considerable distances, until they are trapped in some hollow or against a rock, where they become buried by wind-blown sand. When rain falls, it collects in these hollows, so the seeds have favourable conditions for germination.

Rolling plants of the desert include tumbleweeds, and the well-known Rose of Jericho (*Anastatica hierochuntica*). At the beginning of the hot season, its fruits mature, the leaves fall off, and the dry branches roll inwards to form a wickerwork basket. This protects the seed pods until the branches uncurl again when next they become damp. The roots are so small that, when the plant is rolled up, it can be blown along like a balloon!

Other plants have evolved mechanisms which do the reverse and restrict seed dispersal. The stems and leaves curl inwards when the air is dry, but open up when it is moist. By this means, seeds are scattered only during the rainy season, and germinate near to the parent plant which is already growing in a favourable locality. So, plants either prevent their seeds from dispersing, or else distribute them as far as

possible. There are no half measures!

Perennial grasses, shrubs and bushes which live for a long time, need to be able to survive through months or years of drought without suffering injury. Some, like the Creosote Bush (*Larrea divaricata*) of North America, have leaves which can become completely dried out and yet retain the power to recover and grow when rain comes again.

Most desert plants, however, do not tolerate becoming dried up in this way. Instead, they resist drought and keep their moisture from evaporating. Their leaves are often coated with wax which prevents water from evaporating through them. Some are covered with hairs or spines, which not only reduce evaporation but also reflect the heat from the sun. Many trees drop their leaves at the beginning of the dry season, while other plants, like cacti and switch-plants, are always leafless. Some plants only have small leaves, while the blades of desert grasses are rolled into tubes with the air pores or 'stomata' opening into them. The leaves of acacias fold up at night. This greatly reduces the evaporation of water at a time when it is not necessary for cooling the leaves.

Most drought-resisting desert plants have very deep roots. The rooting systems of mesquite and acacia trees, for example, may go down to a depth of 15 metres (50 feet) or more. These long tap roots can reach moisture far below the surface of the soil. At the same time, a network of shallow roots traps the water from showers and thunderstorms. Especially in cool coastal deserts, fog and dew collect at night on the leaves

Top:
A Cape Ground Squirrel investigating ephemeral flowers after a rainstorm in the Kalahari desert.

Above:
A creosote bush of the North American deserts, festooned with seed pods some weeks after rain has fallen.

having a small surface-to-volume ratio helps animals of cold deserts to conserve their heat, so it helps cacti to retain their moisture. It has been said that even a small cactus would lose water several hundred times faster if it were divided up into leaves having the same total weight. The fluted stems of the giant saguaro and candelabra cactuses of Mexico and Arizona, whose branches tower to heights of more than 18 metres (60 feet), expand and contract like accordians as moist and dry seasons alternate. Cacti are native to the New World but, long ago, they were introduced into the Great Palaearctic desert, the Kalahari, and the Australian desert where the Prickly Pear (*Opuntia inermis*) became a major pest. No one really knows who first brought the prickly pear to Australia. There is a story that a former Governor did so to provide food for the cochineal insects that feed on it. He wanted cochineal insects so that he could use their scarlet dye for the tunics of his soldiers! But this is probably untrue. It seems more likely that the cacti were first brought in as ornamental plants.

At first, the cacti did no harm, and nobody heard much of the prickly pear until farmers began to use it for hedges in the 1860s. Then the trouble started and, by 1900, cacti were becoming a real nuisance, for they prevented the land from being grazed by sheep. Within a few years, much of Queensland was covered with an impenetrable wall of spiny cactus, and the cost of clearing it would greatly have exceeded the value of the land itself! In 1927, however, a moth was introduced into Australia the caterpillars of which ate prickly pear. The moth increased so quickly that, three years later, the cactus was almost completely destroyed and the land could again be used for farming. The control of a weed or pest by another animal is known as 'biological control'. It is cheap and can be very effective. Unfortunately it does not always work, so expensive insecticides or herbicides have to be used, and these may be harmful to the environment.

Succulent plants are not found only in deserts. They also occur in temperate regions where the soil is saline – as in salt-marshes and on the seashore. Although there may be abundant moisture in such places, plants cannot easily absorb it because of its high sodium chloride (salt) content. Tamarisks, however, absorb saline water through their roots and eliminate the surplus salt through special glands on the surface of their leaves.

The ability to grow in saline places depends not only upon the concentration of the salt, but also on the kind of salt present. Some desert soils contain sodium chlorate. This is the same chemical that gardeners use as a weedkiller. No plants can grow in places where it is found, although water

and stems of plants, and the water trickles down to the sand where it is collected by shallow roots.

Several kinds of iris and lily plants avoid the hot dry season of the desert altogether, not as resistant seeds, but as dormant bulbs, tubers, or fleshy roots. From these grow stems, leaves and flowers – after rain has fallen. These plants have no need for water storage, since they are active only when the soil is wet.

Plants that store water

Although cacti and euphorbias have shallow roots, they can store considerable quantities of water for use during the dry season. Because of their large size and compact shape, they have small surface areas compared with their volumes. Just as containing sodium chlorate can be drunk by Man and by animals without harm. On the other hand, plants can absorb water containing so much magnesium sulphate that it affects animals like a strong dose of Epsom salts. Although soda – sodium carbonate – is itself no more harmful to plants than ordinary salt, it clogs the soil, so that water and air cannot penetrate to the roots.

Specializations for survival

Many desert trees and shrubs are extremely prickly, with painfully sharp thorns and spikes. They need to be, because food is scarce, and thorns help to protect them from browsing and grazing animals. Other plants have poisonous or bitter sap. Only the silliest goat would go on eating senna pods after one or two trials! Creosote bushes have an unappetising smell, while Sodom apples contain sticky white latex which is so poisonous that the plants are eaten only by one kind of grasshopper. This, in turn, absorbs so much poison from its food that it is never preyed on by lizards, mice or birds.

The advantages to be gained from poisons and spines are not absolute. You cannot make your home absolutely secure from burglars, but you can make it so difficult to break into that they will not bother to try. Instead, they rob someone else. Similarly, although one species of grasshopper has specialized in eating Sodom apple, camels, goats and gazelles will not touch it. Because the thorns of an acacia do not protect it entirely from browsing animals or from nibbling caterpillars and locusts, it does not follow that the tree is not protected to some extent from these and other animals that might otherwise eat it all up.

Some desert shrubs contain aromatic substance whose smell humans enjoy. These include frankincense and myrrh, which are mentioned in the Bible. Their basic function is probably to make the shrubs unattractive to leaf-eating insects. These substances are produced in greatest concentration at the time when the buds burst – that is, at the beginning of the rainy season. Unlike other insects which avoid them, desert locusts are stimulated by these aromatic compounds, and become sexually mature. Consequently, they are ready to lay their eggs as soon as rain has fallen. It is vitally important that not a moment should be wasted for the young locusts, called hoppers, need to make the fullest use of the ephemeral vegetation which springs up so rapidly, and dies so quickly after rain has fallen. Locusts use the frankincense plants as clocks, and so are prepared for the rainy season when it begins.

The vegetation of desert regions is of three different kinds. Some plants survive on rain and subterranean dew alone. Others grow in depressions and on the edges of wadis where rainwater is concentrated. It is

Above:
Encrusting lichens on a rock in the high tundra of central Alaska during the summer.

Below:
Striped Pyxie toadlets (*Pyxiecephalus delalandii*) safely completing their metamorphosis in liquid mud before their rain-puddle dries out completely.

The dwarf shrubs of the tundra – birch, willow and ling – grow very slowly indeed. A juniper bush, with a stem only 83 millimetres (3·3 inches) thick, had 544 annual rings, and a spruce 60 centimetres (2 feet) thick had more than 400. The wide-spread 'reindeer moss' which, in fact, is a lichen, grows only from 1 to 5 millimetres (0·04 – 0·2 inches) in a year. If it is overgrazed by caribou or reindeer, it takes centuries to recover.

Most tundra plants form low tussocks or rosettes, so that their shoots are protected from the bitter winds after the blanket of snow has been removed. Many survive the winter as bulbs and rhizomes, or underground stems. The few flowering plants produce berries which are eaten by many birds and mammals including the Grizzly Bear (*Ursus horribilis*). Their leaves have leathery, waxy or hairy surfaces which reduce evaporation, like those of many hot desert plants.

'Ephemeral' animals

The appearance of the tundra is completely transformed when the snow melts. The air fills with humming insects and there are so many bloodsucking blackflies and mosquitoes about that travellers have to wear special clothing. These vast hordes of hungry insects themselves provide abundant food for the migratory birds that fly to the Arctic regions each year to breed.

A similar hum of activity is heard when the rains come to alleviate the drought and heat of tropical and subtropical deserts. Swarms of locusts breed in the damp sand and the ephemeral vegetation is devoured by hordes of caterpillars and crickets, while the air buzzes with a rare abundance of flies, wasps and beetles. Scorpions and camel spiders gorge themselves on all this food, so briefly plentiful. Migratory birds appear and build their nests, while most resident reptiles, birds and mammals produce their young at this time.

So greatly is the desert transformed that hollows become shallow pools filled with tadpole shrimps, brine shrimps and other crustaceans, aquatic insects and the tadpoles of desert toads. How do these animals exist during the long dry season of the year? Just as ephemeral plants survive in the form of drought-resistant seeds, so do crustaceans and many insects pass the dry season as dormant eggs. The life of such an animal is a veritable race against time for it must hatch, grow up, and lay eggs before the desert pool dries up. A tadpole shrimp can grow from a microscopic egg to a mature crustacean over 2.5 centimetres (1 inch) long, in the brief span of 10 days!

Such creatures only survive because there are no fishes in the temporary rain pools to snap them up before they have time to reproduce. True, some may be eaten by

in places such as this that agricultural crops can best be grown without irrigation. Thirdly, vegetation may depend upon moisture coming from sources beyond the desert. The plants and trees of oases, those that grow beside rivers, and those that are irrigated artificially, belong to this category.

Plants of polar deserts

The plants of polar deserts are similarly restricted to favourable localities. Around the poles, there is perpetual frost, the growth of vegetation is impossible, and animals have to depend upon the seas for their food. Where the soil thaws in summer, however, plants are able to grow – although trees are only found in river valleys. In general, mosses, lichens and heaths predominate, along with dwarf birches and willows.

The long period of frost, followed by an extremely short growing season, only allows a few very hardy plants to survive. The vegetation is generally greenish-grey in colour, because of the lichens which are so plentiful. This type of country is known as *tundra*, from a Finnish word which means an unforested hill. It is not found much in the southern hemisphere because the land masses taper to narrow points. Only two species of flowering plants have been found on the edges of the ice-covered Antarctic continent.

Much of the tundra overlies deep deposits of dead sphagnum moss, which does not decompose because it is too cold. The ice only melts to a depth of a few centimetres. Most plants spread feverishly during the short growing season, and do not set seed at all. When seeds are produced, however, they are extremely resistant to frost. Seeds of Arctic lupins have been found to germinate successfully, after being buried and permanently frozen for at least 10,000 years!

spoonbills, flamingoes and other birds but, in general, they have relatively few enemies. When there is not enough rain for the desert pools to remain long enough for the tadpole shrimps to reproduce, the young shrimps must perish before laying their eggs. This does not prove to be a disaster for these crustaceans, however, because some eggs hatch only after two, three, or even more immersions. Consequently, there will still be plenty of survivors when a heavy fall of rain occurs.

In northern Nigeria and Kenya, there are certain desert midges whose larvae inhabit small pools formed in shallow hollows on the tops of rocks and boulders. Every time these hollows dry up, the larvae dry up too, and remain dormant until it rains again. They can survive remarkable extremes of temperature, but only when their tissues have dried out completely. It is even possible to cut one of them in half and leave it for several years. When the two halves are wetted, they will wriggle for a moment and then die from the injury inflicted so long before!

The desert dries up remarkably quickly after the rain has ceased to fall. Flowering plants bloom, shed their seeds, wither and die. Gone are the insects that assumed temporary abundance on the short-lived vegetation. Gone, too, are the huge camel spiders that preyed on them. Underneath rocks, and down holes in the ground you may find a few scorpions and insect larvae but, except for ants and black darkling beetles, adult insects have become very scarce.

Above:
Barren Ground Caribou pause to graze on a river bank while migrating through central Alaska.

Below left:
Tundra vegetation in Alaska during the short summer growing season.

Below:
A dense growth of green grass and other vegetation that has sprung up in the Kalahari after abnormally heavy rain.

27

Scorpions, spiders and insects

Below:
Woodlice of arid regions are able to reduce the amount of water lost through evaporation not only by their large size, but also by rolling into a ball.

Bottom:
Droplets of moisture deposited by fog in the cool coastal dunes of the Namib desert are eagerly sucked up by ants.

Bottom right:
The Whip Scorpion or Vinegaroon of south-western North America is able to eject a spray of acetic acid to deter predatory enemies.

The aquatic creatures we have been talking about mostly belong to a class called the crustaceans. They are not proper desert animals, for only their eggs are adapted to withstand drought and heat. Crustaceans form part of a group of animals known as arthropods. The name means 'jointed legs', and the legs, like the rest of the body, are protected by a hard external skeleton, or 'cuticle'. This is fairly porous in crustaceans, so they are not really adapted to withstand desert climates. Better adapted are two other groups of arthropods – spiders and their relations, and insects. Some

people mistakenly think that spiders are insects, but the two are quite distinct. Insects have six legs; spiders have eight. The body of an insect is divided into head, thorax and abdomen, that of a spider is in only two parts. Insects have antennae, a pair of large, compound eyes and usually wings. Spiders have no antennae or wings. They have six or eight simple eyes, and spinnerets from which they weave their silk. Alongside the jaws are a pair of leg-like limbs called pedipalps.

Spiders are related to scorpions, whip scorpions, harvest spiders, camel spiders, ticks and mites. These, and other lesser-known eight-legged arthropods, form the group of animals called arachnids. Just as a beetle and a fly are both insects, so a spider and a scorpion are arachnids. Centipedes and millipedes are two other arthropod groups. All arthropods are small and so have large surface-to-volume ratios.

Desert crustaceans

Most crustaceans are aquatic, living in freshwater or the sea. The only ones that live permanently on land are woodlice. There are two ways in which an arthropod, with its relatively huge surface area, can survive on land without drying up. One is to stay most of the time in a damp place. This is what woodlice, centipedes and millipedes do. You can find them under stones and fallen leaves, under the bark of trees and in the soil, where it is damp. In desert regions, they can only survive where there is mois-

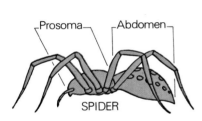

SPIDER

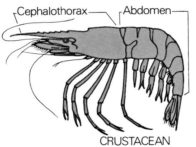

CRUSTACEAN

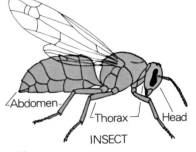

INSECT

ture – in oases, under rocks, or buried deeply in the sand. Even so, they are usually not common.

There is, however, a large desert woodlouse, found throughout North Africa and the Middle East, which makes deep holes in the fine sand where wadi beds discharge into open plains. These woodlice are social, and work in pairs to dig the burrows down which they live. They are quite big – about 2 centimetres (0·8 inches) long – and run rapidly with their bodies held well above the hot surface of the ground. During the hottest part of the day, none of them can be seen, but, at dusk and dawn they emerge to feed upon plant material and, sometimes, on each other. When I measured the temperature inside their holes, I found that deep down, there was a time lag of several hours so that the maximum temperature there was reached long after the temperature on the surface of the sand had dropped. Consequently, the animals were actually emerging from hotter to cooler conditions although the sun had not yet set.

Nocturnal animals that spend the daytime hidden in cool, damp, burrows cannot see that the sun is setting. How, then, can they tell that the time has come for them to leave their retreats? The answer is that they possess a sense of time, a biological clock, just as we do. Many people are able to judge the passing of time very accurately, even when they are asleep, and can wake just before their alarms have been set to wake them. In the same way, night-active animals wake up and come out when the sun sets.

Below:
A North American Desert Scorpion (*Hadrurus arizonensis*) which digs unusually deep burrows.

Bottom:
A large black scorpion (*Heterometrus* species) from damper regions of Southern India.

Unlike woodlice and centipedes, insects and arachnids are able to live in very dry places. In order to do this, they have to be completely waterproof. Their cuticles are covered with an impervious layer of wax through which little or no water vapour can evaporate. At the same time, although they need to breathe, the openings to the respiratory organs are normally kept closed by special muscles. Only when carbon dioxide begins to accumulate in the body, are they opened to allow oxygen to enter and carbon dioxide to pass out.

Land-living arthropods are all rather small. None of them can afford to use water for the excretion of urine. Consequently, waste products are eliminated as dry, insoluble crystals. Water is also removed from the undigested material passing through the gut so that none is lost in this way either. The ways in which water is saved and economized by all terrestial arthropods are especially well developed among the inhabitants of tropical and subtropical deserts.

Arachnids of the sands

Among small animals, scorpions are, perhaps, most symbolic of the desert. Like woodlice, scorpions are strictly nocturnal in habit and spend the day in sheltered retreats under rocks and stones or down deep burrows which they dig with their claws. Unlike woodlice, however, they are covered with a thin layer of hard, impervious wax which gives them a shiny appearance. This renders them extremely resistant to water loss. Why, then, are they only active at night? The answer, I think is that they are rather large animals and therefore vulnerable to predatory enemies. Although they have poisonous stings to protect them from enemies, these would have little effect against the strong talons of a hawk and they would be quickly snapped up by the long beak of a stork if they were to wander in the open during the daytime when they could easily be seen.

Scorpions feed entirely on other animals, mostly insects. They do not usually go to seek their food, but wait for their prey to enter their lair in order to hide. When hungry, however, they emerge at night and walk about with claws extended. They have poor eyesight but a very delicate sense of touch which lies in the long hairs which project from their claws. When they come in contact with an insect prey, they grab it so quickly that it has little chance of escaping. Then, if it struggles, it is stung.

There are two types of scorpion poison. One is local in effect and comparatively harmless to Man. The stings of the small black scorpions of southern Europe and of the very large black scorpions of tropical Africa, for instance, are no worse than a bee sting. The venoms of the yellow desert scorpions, on the other hand, are nerve poisons. They also destroy red blood corpuscles. They are as toxic as the venom of a cobra, although the quantity injected is usually much smaller.

Like other poisonous animals, some species of scorpion make hissing noises when disturbed. There is no evidence that scorpions, any more than snakes, can hear the warning sounds that they themselves produce. The presence of sound-producing organs implies a sense of hearing, not in the performers themselves but in the enemies that might otherwise attack them.

Although they cannot hear airborne sounds, scorpions, like snakes, are very sensitive to vibrations of the ground. It seems that their hearing organs are a pair of sensory, comb-like structures on the underneath of the body near the bases of the legs. These organs have other functions as well – they are used to determine whether the ground over which a scorpion is walking is suitable for mating. Let me explain. On finding a female, the male scorpion grasps her claws in his and dances backwards and forwards, holding hands with his mate. When he crosses a rock or some other firm object, which he detects with his 'combs', he deposits a spermatophore on it. A

spermatophore is a small packet containing sperms, at the end of a long stalk. Then he manoeuvres the female so that the spermatophore is taken into her body, where the eggs are fertilized. The young scorpions are born alive. Until their first moult, they are plump and weak, but ride in safety on their mother's back.

Above:
A female Tailless Whip Scorpion (*Admetus* species) of Trinidad with young.

Below:
Courtship in scorpions consists of a dance during which the male deposits a spermatophore and manoeuvres the female over it.

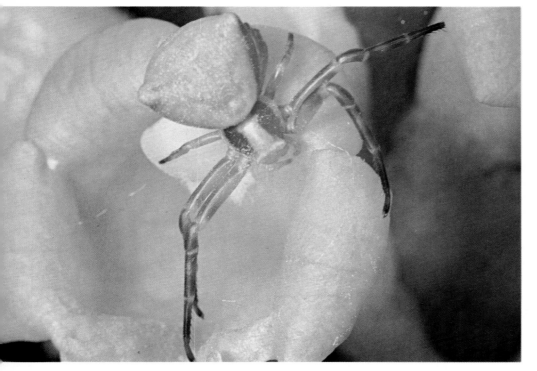

Even more than scorpions, camel spiders or jerrymanders are typical animals of the desert. Amongst the largest of the arachnids, camel spiders are familiar to all who have travelled in arid regions. These creatures avoid fertile oases and seem to prefer utterly neglected places where the soil is broken and bare. Sometimes they can be seen running so fast that they resemble balls of yellow thistledown blowing over the desert. Often, when going at full speed, they will stop abruptly and begin hunting about like a dog that has caught the scent of game.

Camel spiders are nocturnal, and hide away in deep burrows or under stones during the daytime. They are extremely voracious carnivores and will continue feeding until their abdomens are so distended they can scarcely move. Almost any insect, spider, scorpion or other camel spider, as well as small lizards, birds or mice are attacked and devoured. Their adaptations to desert life include considerable powers of water conservation, the ability to tolerate extremes of drought and temperature, nocturnal habits and the possession of good biological clocks.

As in scorpions, the mating of camel spiders involves the transfer of a spermatophore from the male to the female. Courtship is brief and a ball of sperms is inserted directly by the male without being fixed first to the ground. The eggs are usually laid at night, and hatch within a day or two. The young are guarded by the mother until after their first moult, but they do not climb onto her back.

Desert spiders are usually white or pale in colour, and lack the darker markings found among their relatives that live in humid climates. Some of them have brushes of hairs on the undersides of their limbs which help them to walk on sand. One of the larger hunting spiders inhabiting the Namib desert digs a tube in the sand and cements the grains with a criss-cross of webbing. Loose sand is pushed up the slope of the tube by the mouthparts of the spider. Other species live on the trunks of acacia trees and bushes.

Crab spiders lie in wait for their insect prey on the ground or in vegetation. They usually match their background so closely as to be almost invisible. Some species can change colour quite quickly.

Jumping spiders are small animals with broad, square heads, extremely large eyes and short, stout legs. They have very keen sight and stalk their prey from afar, whereas wolf spiders hunt in the open and overcome their prey by sheer speed and strength. They have longer bodies and limbs but their eyes are smaller. Orb-web

Left:
The wolf spider has excellent vision and runs down its prey with sheer speed and strength.

Below left:
The White Lady Spider of the Namib desert digging its silk-lined burrow.

Below:
These Giant Red Velvet Mites (*Dinothrombium* species) are found in desert regions throughout the world. Their bright colour is a warning that they are distasteful to predators and even camel spiders will not eat them.

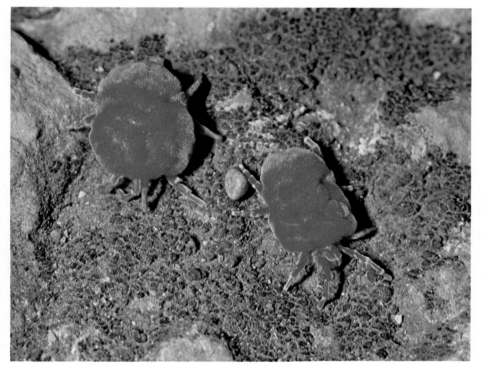

spiders usually attach their snares to vegetation. These spiders have an irregular shape which, combined with their sandy colour, makes them very inconspicuous.

Spiders do not produce spermatophores. When the male reaches maturity he weaves a small pad of silk on which he deposits a drop of sperm. He then sucks this up with his pedipalps which, in due course, are inserted into the body of the female. The courtship of spiders is very interesting. It is of utmost importance to the male to establish his identity so that the female does not treat him like an insect victim. Consequently, whichever of the senses is the one on which the species.chiefly relies for the capture of its prey is the sense most employed in courtship. For instance, male jumping spiders and wolf spiders make use of visual signs and wave their pedipalps or legs. Short-sighted and nocturnal spiders stroke each other, while male web-spinners use distinctive tweaks and vibrations of the threads of the female's snare.

Mites are sometimes found in desert soils, but they are not numerous. Adult giant velvet mites often appear in the deserts of Africa and America a week or two after rain, and probably feed on termites and other insects. The larvae are parasitic on grasshoppers. A high rate of water loss indicates that they are not particularly well adapted to drought. They dig burrows where the sand is damp. Their scarlet coloration has a warning function and is associated with glands which render them distasteful to enemies such as scorpions and camel spiders. In contrast, many species of tick are well adapted to life in arid places. When not attached to their hosts, these

Above:
The Desert Locust (*Schistocerca gregaria*) of Africa and the Middle East forms vast swarms of up to 10,000 million insects which eat their own weight of food in a day leaving famine in their wake.

Opposite, top and inset:
Termites do well in arid regions because most of their lives are spent beneath the surface of the ground.

Opposite, right:
Earwigs are successful desert insects. The species shown (*Forficula senegalensis*) is found along the edge of the Sahara.

Opposite, far right:
Larva and pupa of an Ant-lion (*Morter obscurus*). The pupa is lying in its cocoon which has been opened to show the insect inside.

animals show remarkable powers of water conservation and some can live for 10 years or more without food or drink. The ticks of goats and camels are extremely common throughout the Great Palaearctic desert. Some of the larger kinds are notorious for their vicious bite and can cause quite serious loss of blood to their host.

Swarms of insects

Insects, like arachnids, are covered with a layer of hard wax so that some of them are able to live in the desert without losing too much water by evaporation. Moreover, the waste products eliminated from the body are so dry that the amount of moisture wasted is negligible. In contrast to arachnids, desert insects are mostly herbivorous and only a few of the many kinds are predatory. Bristletails are abundant in the Namib desert and other extremely arid regions where they feed on dry vegetation. Crickets, locusts and grasshoppers are found in most desert regions, and may become very numerous at the time of rain.

Locust swarms often comprise 10,000 million insects, travel up to 3,000 kilometres (1,900 miles) in a season, and eat their own weight of food in a day. The desert locust is a constant threat to agriculture in the Great Palaearctic desert. After the locusts have flown away, the people are left to starve unless famine relief can be brought to them. Locusts and other grasshoppers show little adaptation to the desert environment, but some crickets have combs of long hairs on their back legs which help them to walk across sand.

Many plant-sucking bugs live in the desert, feeding on the sparse vegetation. Mealy bugs are fairly numerous in desert areas and the 'manna' which sustained the Israelites during their wanderings in Sinai, was the secretion of one of them. Another bug, which occurs in arid parts of South America, becomes completely covered with a waxy coating inside which it can resist prolonged drying for up to 17 years. As soon as it is put into damp soil, however, it begins to absorb moisture and continues its development.

Tropical termites usually build their mounds in a north-south direction so that a comparatively small area of the nest is exposed to the midday sun. Dead shrubs in the Sonoran desert and elsewhere are usually eaten away by wood-eating termites. Other termites make their nests at the bases of living agaves, ocotillo, cholla and other cacti. In the more arid deserts, only soil-dwelling termites occur. Although earwigs are nearly always found in moist situations in temperate regions, some of the larger species are equally at home in quite arid places. Earwigs are nocturnal, and hide under stones and down cracks in the soil during the day.

Ant lions, whose larvae have been called 'demons of the dust', are characteristic insects of hot deserts during the summer season. Their cone-shaped pits can be seen especially well in fine sand. At the bottom of each pit lies buried an ant lion larva, in ambush for passing ants and other insects that may slide into the trap. The prey is knocked down by particles of sand flicked with surprising force and accuracy by the larva waiting below.

Bees require nectar and pollen and their activity is therefore restricted to the rainy season, but wasps and ants are common desert insects. Most wasp species excavate holes in sandy soil where they deposit the paralyzed spiders and insects which serve as food for their larvae. The majority of ants live in underground nests, although a few nest in the wood of dead trees or under bark. Most species live in comparatively moist localities, and only a few are found in really arid soils. One even brings water to its nest from salty, damp sand deep underground. Harvester ants are affected by

Below:
Robber-flies (*Asilidae*) prey on other insects. Desert species, which are quite common, are usually black in colour.

extremes of heat and cold, but live in deep nests and forage only during a brief period each day, when the temperature is favourable.

Butterflies and moths of the desert do not at first appear to show any special adaptations. A behavioural adaptation is to remain flying within the shelter of a small bush, even when the wind is raging outside. Hairy caterpillars are sometimes blown along by the wind, rolled up into a ball, while the larvae of certain species in America inhabit long tubes of sand attached to the stems of plants.

Flies, including the common House Fly (*Musca domestica*), are all too plentiful in the desert, especially near oases. Among the many other kinds are sandflies, craneflies, hover-flies, and long-snouted bee-flies which suck nectar. Robber flies are not uncommon while blood-sucking horseflies constantly attack camels, horses or donkeys. One of the bot-flies develops parasitically in the nose of the camel. The mature larva is sneezed out on to the sand where it continues its development.

Beetles are characteristic of desert life and darkling beetles are particularly well adapted. Second to these come dung beetles and burying beetles, while blister beetles, ground beetles and tiger beetles are also common. The well-known Egyptian sacred scarab beetle acts as a scavenger by breaking up and burying the droppings of camels, goats and other animals. Many

American scarab beetles have become secondarily adapted to eating vegetation and fallen leaves. Some of them may burrow to a depth of 3 metres (10 feet) or more in the soil.

Predatory beetles are often found in dung or carrion where they prey on the maggots and other insect larvae developing there. Blister beetles, on the other hand, are herbivores. They secrete a disagreeable, oily fluid from the joints of their limbs, which raises painful blisters on the skin. The adults possess conspicuous coloration, vivid black and green, brown or blue and red which acts as a warning. Tiger beetles and ground beetles are predatory, both as larvae and adults. The former seldom take to the wing, but the latter are skilful fliers, common on sand on the banks of rivers and temporary rainpools, or beside the sea. The larvae inhabit tubes in the sand from which they watch for passing prey. One American species cements the sand grains with saliva, and the burrow serves as a pitfall to trap other insects. Many of the desert ground beetles are wingless.

Black darkling beetles are common throughout all the deserts of the world. They are able to live on dry food without any water. The majority of them are nocturnal, but one or two species may be day-active, except in extremely hot conditions when they burrow in the sand. Some species of the Namib desert have exceptionally long legs, while others have very short

legs adapted for burrowing. The commonest American darkling beetles are often active during the hottest parts of the day. Most darkling beetles do not have wings, and their wing-cases are fused together, leaving an air-space beneath. This not only serves for purposes of insulation, keeping their bodies cool during the day and warm at night, but is of even greater importance in reducing the amount of water lost by evaporation, for the breathing holes open into it. Darkling beetles are omnivorous, feeding on vegetable matter, carrion and dung.

Above:
Darkling beetles (*Tenebrionidae*) are common in desert regions. They are usually black in colour but a few species are sandy.

Below:
Blister Beetles (*Mylabris pustulata*) protect themselves from enemies by secreting an oily fluid which raises painful blisters on the skin.

Opposite bottom:
Leaf-eating beetles are often brightly coloured. They feed on the tissues of plants in most parts of the world, including deserts.

Insects are the most numerous arthropods in cold deserts. Arachnids are almost absent – except for a few spiders, harvest spiders and mites. Whereas beetles are the most common insects in other parts of the world, flies are by far the most numerous in the Arctic tundra. Many kinds of mosquitoes, blackflies and deerflies abound, and suck the blood of caribou, musk-oxen, moose and Man.

Insects usually survive the cold winter either in the egg state, or as hibernating adults. They can tolerate very low temperatures, either because their blood contains glycerol which acts as an anti-freeze, or because they become desiccated. Then they can freeze solid without water forming crystals in their tissues and harming them.

Snails

Apart from arthropods, the only other animals without backbones to be found in the desert are snails. In Israel, North Africa, parts of Arabia, and California, for instance, where drought is not too intense, snails are quite common. During the dry season, they remain sealed up inside their shells in a state of suspended animation. In this way they can survive for several years. A spectacular example is afforded by two specimens of *Eremina desertorum* which were glued to appropriate supports and exhibited in the British Museum (Natural History) from March 1846 to March 1850, when one revived and fed. Two others, collected in Egypt in May, 1854, were still alive five

years later, and some specimens of *Otala lactea* from a region of the Sahara where there had been no rain for five years, were kept dry in a bottle for another three and a half years and then recovered when provided with water!

When rain falls, desert snails wake up, feed and reproduce; and when dry conditions return again they hide away among

rocks or down cracks in the ground. They feed on the fresh green leaves that spring up after rain. The snail's foot fixes its body to the ground while the animal propels itself along by waves of muscular contraction and relaxation. Slime is first secreted by the animal on to the sand or rock, and provides a track along which the animal glides. Since the trail remains long after the snail has moved away, there is no tendency for small sand grains to stick to the snail's foot. Slime on the upper surface of the body helps to prevent evaporation. Because their moist bodies would freeze solid, snails are not found in polar deserts. The Giant Snails of the hot West African deserts have, however, been introduced into many other parts of the world because of their food value.

Left:
African Giant Snails (*Achatina* species) emerging during the rains. They are good to eat and are dried, smoked and sold in markets.

Amphibians, reptiles and birds

Vertebrates are animals with backbones. Arthropods and snails are invertebrates, and do not have internal bony skeletons. Vertebrates are usually much larger than invertebrates, so their surface-to-volume ratios are smaller. This means that the tendency for them to dry out is less marked, and the very largest desert mammals, like camels and antelopes, can even afford to cool their bodies by the evaporation of sweat.

The vertebrates include fishes, amphibians, reptiles, birds and mammals. Wherever there are permanent waters, fishes can be found. Desert fishes often have to withstand high temperatures, marked changes in salinity, muddy waters, and other adverse conditions. But they are, nevertheless, fishes. They live in water and are therefore not true desert animals. The fishes of polar regions need to be adapted to life in very cold seawater. At the same time, there is ample food in the sea, so they grow well. Much of the animal life of the Arctic, and almost all Antarctic animals, depend upon the fishes of the sea for their food.

Amphibians

Amphibians – newts and salamanders, frogs and toads – cannot be successful desert animals because they need water in which to breed. A number of toads do, however, manage to maintain themselves in the arid tropics and subtropics. Their adaptations include reduction in water loss

Opposite:
A Mourning Dove on its nest in Cholla Cactus, Arizona. Mourning Doves are better able than most birds to survive in conditions of heat and drought.

Below:
The African Toad (*Bufo regularis*) manages to survive on the fringes of the Sahara and Kalahari deserts.

from heat and drought. There are a few Australian desert frogs which emerge from their burrows even in hot dry weather. Although they feed at night, they lose more water by evaporation than they gain with their food. The difference is made up by absorbing moisture during the day from the damp soil in the burrow. Amphibians do not normally drink, but take up water through their skins. In polar deserts amphibians are never found because the ice does not melt for long enough for them to breed at such low temperatures.

Cold-blooded creatures in a hot climate

In contrast to amphibians, reptiles are widely distributed throughout the deserts of the world. Although reptiles are cold-blooded, and so cannot live in really cold conditions, adders are found in Europe as far north as the Arctic Circle, and garter snakes have been recorded in Alaska. These snakes hibernate, spending the winter in deep burrows. Both species produce their young alive. Reptile eggs could not develop outside the mother because of low air temperatures and the shortness of summer. By basking in any available sunshine, however, snakes whose eggs develop inside the mother's body, are able to find enough warmth for the young to be born alive before the end of the summer. Unlike birds

Below:
Desert lizards, like this agamid, hold their bodies high above the hot surface. *Inset:* Temperature regulating behaviour. A. Warming its head and brain in the morning before emerging from the sand. B. In shade during the heat of the day. C. In the open but angled to reduce the amount of solar heat it receives.

by evaporation, and increased uptake of water after they have suffered from drought. The eggs of desert toads, which breed in temporary rainpools, are able to develop extremely rapidly. The tadpoles would die if they were stranded on land. In dry weather, desert toads bury themselves deep in the soil where they are protected

and mammals, most of whose body heat is obtained from the digestion and breakdown of food, reptiles depend for heat mainly on sunning themselves. When warm enough, they move into shade and so are able to keep a reasonably constant body temperature.

Reptiles are well adapted for desert life. Their skin is thick, scaly and comparatively impervious, so that they lose little water by evaporation through it. Urinary wastes are eliminated as a pulpy, or semi-solid mass, containing very little water. Lizards are the most successful of desert reptiles. Most species feed on insects and spiders whose blood provides them with water. Some, however, in particular the scaly-tailed lizards of the Great Palaearctic desert, are mainly herbivorous. In these, the short, thick tail is covered with whorls of large scales. The body is flattened and the head is smooth and covered with very small scales.

The 'horned toads' of North America also have flattened bodies covered with spiky scales. Desert iguanas are abundant in valleys and plains where creosote bushes occur with rodent holes and burrows under them. Adaptations of these lizards include elongated scales fringing the edges of certain toes and widening them. These serve as sand-shoes and help the lizards to burrow beneath the surface of the sand. Valves prevent the entry of sand into the nose, and the head is wedge-shaped to assist in moving through the sand. The enlarged scales on the sides of the legs and tail also tend to force the animals down into the sand when the limbs are moved. Similar adaptations are found among many other kinds of lizards that inhabit sandy deserts.

The eyes of many sand-dwelling lizards, including skinks and geckos, have a remarkable window in the lower eyelid. In some, this takes the form of a circular, transparent disc which occupies the whole eyelid. Consequently the lizard is able to see although its eyes are permanently closed with the lids fixed together, thus providing protection from the sand.

Geckos are widespread throughout the tropics and a number of them have become adapted to desert life. Their heads are broad, their bodies flattened and their toes equipped with pads which adhere by means of friction, so that they can run up smooth, vertical surfaces. Some desert geckos have webbed feet for support on loose sand. These animals are active at dusk and during the night, but can withstand considerable desiccation and starvation. One Sahara species can lose over half its body weight without ill effect, and then recover when food is again available. The most imposing of the desert lizards is the Desert Monitor (*Varanus griseus*) which reaches a length of 1.5 metres (5 feet). It is a

Opposite top:
The Regal Horned Lizard (*Phrynosoma solare*) inhabits the foothills of the Sonoran desert. It is day active and does not emerge from its nesting place until it has become warm and fully active.
Above:
The slit-shaped pupil of the eye of this Namib desert gecko closes in sunlight to exclude most of the glare.
Below:
The Nile Monitor (*Varanus niloticus*) is as large or larger than the Desert Monitor (*V. griseus*) but more brightly coloured. It is a powerful, predatory lizard widely distributed throughout Africa even in arid parts.

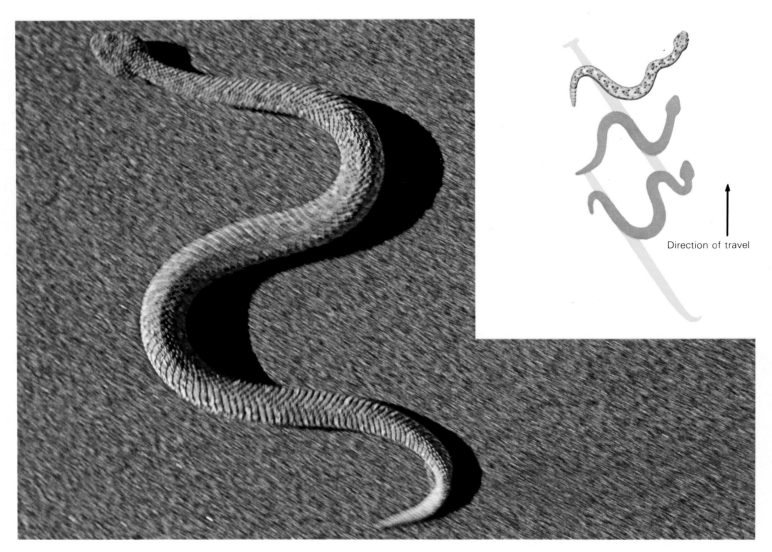

Direction of travel

Above:
Sidewinding movement is found in many desert snakes, like this Namib Desert Viper.

Inset:
In its looping movement, the sidewinder touches the ground in only two places and then unwinds its body until its head is extended enough to touch down for the beginning of another loop. This leaves characteristic furrows in the desert sand.

Opposite top:
The Hog-nosed Viper (*Bothrops ammodytes*), a small species of the Patagonian desert and Argentine pampas, is characterised by a wart-like protuberance on its upturned snout.

Opposite top right:
The Prairie Rattlesnake (*Crotalus confluentus*) is found throughout much of North America from British Columbia into Lower California and eastwards to Nebraska. It is the natural enemy of many destructive rodents.

Opposite bottom:
A juvenile Desert Tortoise (*Gopherus agassizi*) leaving its burrow in the morning.

speedy and rapacious creature which will eat any other animal that it is strong enough to overcome.

Snakes are much less common than lizards in the desert for they cannot withstand heat so effectively. They are all highly specialized meat-eaters. Like lizards, snakes possess relatively impervious skins, and use little water in excreting urinary waste matter. They eat food rich in moisture, and reduce evaporation by remaining in relatively cool and humid burrows during the heat of the day.

Most snakes are non-poisonous. They have no special method of killing their prey, but swallow it alive so that it dies of suffocation. Back-fanged snakes are moderately poisonous and the venom has to be chewed into the wounds made by the teeth.

Dangerously poisonous desert snakes include vipers, rattlesnakes, and cobras. True vipers are confined to the Old World, whereas rattlesnakes and a number of related forms are found mostly in the New World, with a few species in Asia. Both the Horned Viper (*Cerastes cerastes*) of the Great Palaearctic desert and the Sidewinder Rattlesnake (*Crotalus cerastes*) of the Great American desert propel themselves forward by looping their bodies sideways in S-shaped curves. The trail left in the sand is a ladder-like succession of furrows. Such

spiral sidewinding causes the snakes to move sideways in the direction to which the head is pointing. In this way the prey can be approached unnoticed. At the same time, the amount of the snake's body that touches the hot sand is reduced. The prey of desert vipers and rattlesnakes consists mainly of desert rats, jerboas and gerbils.

The Egyptian Cobra (*Naja haje*) can be found throughout Africa as far south as Natal. It seems to prefer dry, sandy places where its brownish coloration blends with the dusty surroundings. A quick, bad tempered snake, it rears up at the slightest disturbance and strikes with loud hisses. It moves its body in a series of horizontal waves which flow continuously from head to tail, and seems to travel without effort.

Like lizards, desert tortoises avoid the heat of the sun by burrowing deeply in the ground. They scrape the earth loose with their forefeet and, turning round, push it away with their shells. Advantage is often taken of holes made by other animals, such as ground squirrels. During the morning and evening, when the air is cool, tortoises warm their bodies by basking in the desert sunshine. They do not normally have to drink because they can obtain enough moisture from the succulent plants on which they feed. They do, however, swallow large quantities of water when they are

thirsty. American desert tortoises exist without water throughout the entire dry season. Their eggs are laid in early summer and hatch within three or four months. Not until about five years after hatching do the young tortoises develop a hard shell, and it takes them about 15 to 20 years to reach maturity.

The 'Greek' Tortoise (*Testudo graeca*) occurs throughout most of the Mediterranean region and Asia Minor, its range extending eastwards as far as Iran. Despite its name, it is not found in Greece. Although they normally feed on juicy plants, these tortoises have been found eating the bitter green fruits of dwarf palms. They spend much of the time basking in the sun, but seek the shade when their body temperature begins to get too high. Always they rise late and retire early, being absolutely day-active in their habits. If the air temperature exceeds 40.5°C (105°F), African desert tortoises maintain their body temperature by producing large quantities of saliva which wets the head, neck and front legs. As it evaporates, cooling takes place. The hind legs are also cooled by the evaporation of urine which is stored for use in emergencies in the very large bladder. The eggs which are hard shelled are laid during the autumn and hatch the following summer at the time of the annual rains.

Birds — big and small

Compared with most of the other animals,
birds show little adaptation for desert life.
Apart from being generally paler in colour,
most desert birds are difficult to distinguish
from their relatives of more humid climates.
The most numerous kinds are insect-eaters,
followed by seed-eaters and, lastly, by
flesh-eaters. Many of the latter feed chiefly
upon reptiles. For example, eagles and
falcons live to a large extent on spiny-tailed
lizards in the Great Palaearctic desert. The
Sonoran White-rumped Shrike (*Lanius lud-
ovicianus*) impales its lizard prey on sharp
thorns, while the North American Road-
runner (*Geococcyx californianus*), a relative
of the cuckoos, regularly feeds on snakes.
So does the African Secretary-bird (*Sagit-
tarius serpentarius*).

Although many kinds of birds have been
seen in desert regions, they are usually
found near drinking water. Where there is
no water within their range of flight, birds
are very scarce — in contrast to reptiles and
small mammals. Loss of water by evaporation is the most serious factor affecting
birds in arid regions. Most birds are active
during the daytime. Because they do not
have burrowing habits, they cannot escape
from the midday heat, even though they
rest in the shade as much as possible. Owls
and nightjars are exceptional in hiding
themselves in rock clefts and fissures during the day.

Most desert birds may be seen feeding
actively early in the morning. Later in the
day, the smaller kinds shelter in trees or in
the shade of rocks, resting with hanging
wings and open beaks. Large species such as
eagles, hawks and vultures, on the other
hand, circle overhead, high in the sky
where the air temperature is considerably
lower than it is near the ground. Flesh-
eating and insect-eating birds obtain plenty
of water with their food. The seed-eaters are
faced with the greatest problem of survival
in the desert. They are helped, however, by
their normal high body temperatures and
the fact that birds excrete a very thick and
concentrated urine, containing only small
amounts of water. Birds lose water much
more rapidly than mammals of comparable
size, however, and can survive only on
very succulent food, or by drinking daily.

Every morning, sandgrouse, which are
related to pigeons, fly distances of up to 30
kilometres (19 miles) from their desert
feeding grounds in order to drink their fill
from water holes and rivers. Huge flocks of
these birds, constantly calling to one another with guttural cries, plummet into the
shallow water, drink for two or three sec-
onds, and then wheel off again into the sky,

their rapidly beating wings twinkling in the sunlight as they go. The male bird is equipped with special water-absorbing feathers. In the breeding season, he ruffles his breast before drinking. When he returns to the nest he moistens the eggs, which prevents them from overheating. Instead of incubating their eggs, most desert birds have to shade them from the scorching sunshine. Only ostrich eggs are large enough to survive unshaded for any length of time. After sandgrouse eggs have hatched, the male bird brings moisture to the young, who pass his wet feathers through their beaks. Until they are old enough to fly, they do not obtain water in any other way. It is curious that the female sandgrouse cannot bring water to the chicks as the male bird does.

The Ostrich (*Struthio camelus*) is not able to obtain shelter from the heat of the day in the way that smaller birds do, because it is too large. Ostriches cannot fly, but they are able to run very fast for long distances. Although they need to drink, or eat very moist food, they can live off salty water. Moreover, they can survive the loss of a quarter of their body weight, which can be replaced in a single drink. Cooling is achieved by panting, but ostriches allow their body temperature to rise several degrees before they begin to pant. In this way, water is not used for evaporative

cooling until this becomes absolutely necessary. The ostrich, a native of Africa and the Middle East, is not entirely a desert bird for it is found throughout Africa wherever the country is open and dry.

Residents and migrants
The birds of the polar desert are of two kinds – those that are resident throughout the year, and those which migrate to warmer places before the cold winter sets in. Indeed, only the hardiest birds are able to

Above:
The Ostrich can run very fast for long distances, live off salty water and eat a wide range of plant materials.

Below:
Variegated Sandgrouse (*Pterocles burchelli*) of the Kalahari drinking from a desert pool.

Inset, below:
Double-banded Sandgrouse (*P. bicinctus*) of southern Africa. Male sandgrouse take water to their chicks by wetting their breast feathers.

Above:
Willow Ptarmigan (*Lagopus lagopus*) on thawing tundra. The amount of white plumage has already been reduced by moulting to summer plumage.

Above right:
Female Willow Ptarmigan with her chicks. In winter these birds dig tunnels in the snow where they find food and shelter.

Opposite, top:
The wings of the Wandering Albatross are constructed for soaring in strong winds.

Opposite, right:
Megallenic Penguins (*Spheniscus magellanicus*) at the water's edge.

remain, and many of these show special adaptations to help them to survive. Ptarmigan and grouse have feathered feet with wide toes so that they can walk on the snow without sinking in. In temperate climates, most birds begin to moult their summer feathers as soon as their young are fledged, but the Arctic summer is so short that this process has to be speeded up. In the Far North, ptarmigan moult three times between June and September, to ensure that they remain inconspicuous at all times. In winter ptarmigan dig tunnels in the snow where they find shelter and food.

The Snowy Owl (*Nyctea scandiaca*) remains white throughout the year. It is quite as large as the Eagle Owl (*Bubo bubo*), but lacks eartufts. It nests on the ground and the young have sooty down. This bird hunts both by day and by night. It is a very fierce species, preying not only on lemmings and other land mammals, but also on waterfowl and even fishes – though its heavily muffled feet seem most unsuited to fishing. As food is in short supply, it cannot afford to be choosy!

All the birds of the Antarctic depend upon the sea for their food. They include penguins, which come ashore to breed, skuas, and albatrosses which nest on land but spend the rest of their lives gliding across the oceans. The seas provide an endless supply of food for marine birds in summer but, on land there is practically nothing for them to eat throughout most of the year. Penguins are able to lay down large stores of fat for the winter because they do not fly and therefore have no problems about weight. They are so well insulated by this fat that, when the sun shines, blood is circulated through their flippers and feet to cool their bodies. In winter, they huddle together for warmth.

Mammals

Above:
Gerbil of the Namib desert eating seeds.

Opposite top:
South African Spring Hare digging a burrow – a refuge in times of danger.

Opposite centre:
The Kangaroo Rat can survive desert temperatures of up to 160°C. It spends the day in its burrow.

Opposite bottom:
Jerboas also live underground, emerging only at night.

Although the desert is a harsh and difficult place to live in, various kinds of animals have found answers to the great problem of desert dwellers – how to keep cool without using up too much water. Mammals have particular difficulties to overcome. Like birds, they are warm blooded, which means that their body temperatures stay at a constant level, rising or falling only if they are ill. They are usually covered with fur which keeps them warm in cold weather. In hot weather, on the other hand, they have to keep cool by panting or sweating – which uses up a lot of water. Although baby mammals get plenty to drink from their

mother's milk, their difficulties begin as soon as they are big enough to look after themselves.

Mammals which are small enough to burrow hide away down their holes during the day and only come out at night when the air is relatively cool. Even so, there may be no water for them to drink. All desert animals have to economize as far as possible in the use of water for excretion, and their urine is extremely concentrated. For example, kangaroo rats and jerboas live entirely on grass seeds, and their only moisture comes from the digestion of this dry food. This means that their kidneys have to be extremely efficient. These animals can even drink seawater and excrete the surplus salt!

Desert rodents

Large numbers of rodents are to be found inhabiting different deserts of the world. Rodents include rats, squirrels and other small mammals which gnaw their food with continually growing incisor teeth. Although often not closely related to one another, desert rodents all look much the same. Except for the Spring-hares (*Pedetes caffer*) of South Africa which are larger, desert rodents tend to be about the size of a small rat. They have short fore limbs for burrowing, and long hind legs for jumping. The body is balanced by a long tail tipped with a tuft of hairs. Because of the open nature of the countryside and the poverty of the vegetation, these animals may have to range widely for food. They are fast because, if threatened by a predator, they may need to regain the safety of their burrows at short notice.

The amount of water lost by evaporation through the lungs is extremely low in desert rodents. Their noses are cool because moisture evaporates when they breathe inwards. Then, when they breathe out, their breath is cooled and consequently does not take away much water vapour.

The American Kangaroo Rat (*Dipodomys deserti*) is nocturnal and stays below ground during the day. Measurements of temperature and humidity recorded in kangaroo rat burrows have shown that the moisture content of the air is from two to five times greater than that of the atmosphere outside. This considerably reduces the rate of evaporation of water from the lungs. If the animals were breathing the air outside their burrows, with its low moisture content, the rate of evaporation from their lungs would exceed the rate at which water is formed during metabolism. Metabolism is the name for the chemical processes, occurring within the body, by which food is broken down to release energy and heat. At the same time, carbon dioxide and water are produced. This takes place in all animals, but very few use so little moisture that metabolic water is sufficient for all their needs. As long as they breathe the damp air in their burrows during the daytime, jerboas and kangaroo rats can manufacture all the water they require.

Like birds, desert rodents do not sweat. Only larger mammals have a surface-to-volume ratio sufficiently low for them to be able to afford to cool their bodies by sweating. If a kangaroo rat were to maintain a normal body temperature when the air temperature was around 40°C (104°F), it would have to lose one fifth of its body weight per hour in sweat, and it would soon die. By remaining in their burrows during

Insets:
Left: Karoo Rat (*Pasatomys banksi*) a small nocturnal burrowing rodent of the Kalahari. *Right:* The North American Pack Rat.

Above:
Kalahari Ground Squirrels are active during the day, but spend the dry season in a dormant state in burrows.

the day, however, kangaroo rats are never exposed to such extremes.

They can, nevertheless, regulate their temperature in emergencies. If the body temperature increases towards the lethal limit of about 42°C (108°F) the animal begins to make a large amount of extra saliva. This trickles onto the fur of the chin, and coat, where it evaporates, resulting in a lowering of temperature. This will keep a kangaroo rat alive for up to half an hour at a temperature that would be fatal for any other small rodent. Of course, because small animals heat up very quickly and there is only a limited amount of water available for saliva, they cannot keep this up for long.

Nevertheless, an animal driven from its burrow by a predator would have a better chance of survival with such a mechanism than without. Clearly, water can be used for heat regulation only in the greatest emergency, and evaporation normally takes place only through the lungs.

The adaptations of African and Asian jerboas to their desert environment are similar to those of American kangaroo rats. They live underground, coming out only at night. Because their urine is concentrated, and the waste products of digestion are quite dry, by eating little and excreting little they can live indefinitely on a diet of dry barley or wheat grains (containing only 11-12 per cent water).

A number of other small rodents are able to live in the desert by subsisting on moist food. North African sand rats live and nest in places where the vegetation consists of succulent plants. These plants are usually extremely salty, but sand rats eat them in great quantities and produce a very concentrated urine, up to four times as strong as seawater. The American pack rats and ground squirrels, which feed on juicy cholla fruits, do not possess the same ability to eliminate large quantities of salt but, nevertheless, excrete a concentrated urine. Pack rats protect their burrows by piling up stones and pieces of prickly cactus outside the entrances.

Among other small rodents of the American deserts are grasshopper mice. These feed almost entirely on insects whose blood provides them with all their water. The Desert Hedgehog (*Paraechinus aethiopicus*) of North Africa also obtains water from its food. The Crest-tailed Marsupial Mouse or Mulgara (*Dasycercus cristicauda*), which inhabits the most arid central parts of Australia and is related to kangaroos and wallabies, lives predominantly on insects, supplemented occasionally by lizards and small rodents. Like grasshopper mice, it is able to excrete urine with a relatively small water content and in common with most other desert dwelling mammals, it is a pale sand colour.

Although many desert hares and rabbits excavate tunnels and burrows, the American jack rabbits remain above ground and have no subterranean retreat. They live in places where no free water is available, and depend upon the moisture obtained with their green food. It is not entirely clear how they can survive in the desert without burrowing, but it seems likely that their very large ears, which have a network of blood vessels, help them to lose heat while the animals are resting in the shade. Large ears are found in many desert animals. The Saharan Hare (*Lepus whytei*) also has ears much larger than those of its relatives of temperate climates, perhaps for the same purpose.

Left:
The Marsupial Mouse, which inhabits the most arid parts of Central Australia, lives mainly on insects and lizards.

Below:
The Black-tailed Jack Rabbit (*Lepus californicus*) does not burrow but its large ears help it to keep cool during the daytime.

Above:
Dingoes were introduced into Australia by the original Aborigine settlers and are now widespread throughout the continent.

Right:
The North American Kit Fox is extremely similar to the Saharan Fennec, shown on page 10 because it, too, inhabits a desert environment.

Desert predators

Little is known about desert carnivores but there is no doubt that they obtain considerable quantities of liquid from the blood of their prey. In addition, they tend to have a more varied diet than their relatives from more temperate regions. Desert carnivores include foxes, jackals, hyenas, coyotes, badgers, skunks, small cats, and the Aus-

tralian Dingo (*Canis dingo*). Of these, only foxes are found in extremely arid regions where there is no water at all for drinking. The delightful Fennec Fox (*Fennecus zerda*) of the Sahara possesses a number of characters which are similar to those found in the American Kit Fox (*Vulpes velox*). The Fennec is much smaller than its relatives from temperate climates and when fully grown, weighs less than one kilogramme. It has well-developed sense organs, large eyes and ears, and spends the day in a deep burrow – thus avoiding extremes of heat. It is a pale sandy colour, and lives mainly on insects, lizards, rodents and dates. Its liking for sweet fruit explains the fable of the fox and the grapes. If they get over-heated, Fennecs pant like dogs. They excrete a highly concentrated urine, and the same is probably true of kit foxes.

Winged mammals

We should not leave the small mammals of the desert without making brief reference to bats. Although they have evolved wings and can fly like birds, bats and birds are not related. Their bodies are covered with hair instead of feathers; they do not lay eggs – their young are born alive and drink their mother's milk – and their wings are formed of naked skin stretched between the arm and four enlarged fingers.

When day-active birds retire to rest, their place in the sky is taken by nocturnal bats. Like birds, bats are unable to burrow because their forelimbs have become delicate wings, so they can only live in desert regions where there are caves or cool rock crevices large enough to give them shelter during the day. Also, insect-eating bats seem to be more dependent on water than are most other small mammals. Dusk at a desert waterhole is often enlivened by clouds of bats, which may have flown from quite distant roosting places, swooping

down to drink as they glide low over the surface of the water.

The larger fruit-eating bats are known as 'flying foxes'. They do not penetrate far into the desert, and are found only in oases and the valleys of rivers where they can obtain food. Bats show no special modification for life in hot dry places, but can live there because they are active at night when the air is comparatively cool. Although they are essentially tropical animals, bats are also found in temperate regions where they hibernate in winter. They do not live in the polar regions because they need a lot of food to keep their tiny bodies warm.

Camels – ships of the desert

Life in the desert is even more difficult for larger mammals, such as camels, oryx, antelopes and gazelles, because they are too big to live in holes in the ground. Of course, they rest in the shade of trees and rocks as much as possible, but they may have to survive in great heat, for long periods without drinking. The camel's hair is very coarse so that, when it sweats, the water evaporates on its skin where the cooling is most effective. Furthermore, the camel stores heat during the day so that sweating does not begin unless its body temperature rises above 41°C (106°F). The excess heat that has been stored is lost during the cool

Above:
Epauletted Fruit Bats (*Epomophorus wahlbergis*) hanging up to roost beneath palm fronds in East Africa.

Below left:
Afar women with a laden camel in the cruel Danakil desert of Ethiopia.

Below:
The camel has lost all but two toes in the course of evolution, but compensates for this deficiency by having a foot expanded by fleshy pads so that it does not sink into the soft sand.

CAMEL'S FOOT

BACTRIAN CAMEL

DROMEDARY OR
ARABIAN CAMEL

Above:
The thick fur, stocky body and short legs of the Bactrian camel are adaptations to the cold winters of Turkestan and the Gobi desert. In contrast, the tall, lanky build and coarse hair on its back – which shelters its skin from the sun's heat – are adaptations of the dromedary to life in hot desert regions.

Opposite, top:
Migratory Springbuck of the Kalahari at one time used to trek in immense herds when food supplies ran low.

Opposite, bottom:
Male Dorcas Gazelle. This Saharan species is one of the smallest gazelles.

of the night. The camel's hump is a fat store which is digested during the dry season when there is not enough grass to eat. If this fat were spread all over the body, it would act as a blanket and make the camel hot. Desert sheep store food reserves in their fat tails for the same reason. The camel produces very concentrated urine and its dung is so dry that it can be used immediately for making a fire!

Although camels have only two toes, these are joined by thick, fleshy pads which prevent them from sinking in soft sand. Camels were first domesticated by man in prehistoric times. There are two kinds: the Arabian Camel, or Dromedary (*Camelus dromedarius*) which is widespread throughout the Middle East, India, and North Africa, and possesses a single hump, and the Bactrian Camel (*Camelus bactrianus*). The latter is a heavily built, two-humped animal which inhabits the deserts of central Asia where the winters are cold. It has a long, dark winter coat, short legs and seldom measures more than 2.1 metres (7 feet) from the ground to the top of the humps. This is about the height of the shoulder in the taller and more slender dromedary.

When moving quickly, camels pace. That is, like giraffes and brown bears, they raise both legs on the same side of the body and advance them simultaneously whilst the weight is supported by the legs of the opposite side. In this way a speed of up to about 8 kilometres (5 miles) per hour may be achieved, but cannot be maintained for more than a few hours.

Camels swallow their food twice over because they chew the cud. Their stomachs have small sacs leading from them which, for centuries, were believed to store water for use when they crossed the desert. This is now known not to be true, but these sacs do contain a digestive fluid. It looks like green pea soup and is quite repulsive. To the desert traveller who has no water, however, any fluid is attractive. Tales of people who have saved their lives by killing their camels to drink the fluid in the stomach sacs may therefore well be true.

Camels tolerate a much greater reduction in body water than most other mammals. They can lose nearly one third of their weight without ill effects. We would die after losing about one eighth of ours. Also, camels drink much faster than we can. We are not able to absorb water so quickly through our stomach walls.

Most mammals lose water steadily in hot, dry air as they sweat, pant or merely breathe. Consequently, their blood gradually becomes thicker until it cannot circulate quickly enough to carry away metabolic heat to the skin. When this happens, the body temperature suddenly rises and 'explosive heat death' results. In camels, explosive heat death is avoided because water is lost from the tissues only, while the blood volume remains fairly constant. Thus, the camel is able to live in desert conditions by economizing in water and by tolerating wide variations in body temperature and water content. In winter, when the air temperature is comparatively low, and water is not needed for heat regulation, camels do not need to drink for several months. In summer, the length of time between drinks depends on how hot the weather is, and the amount of work that the animal is called upon to perform.

Other large mammals
Antelopes and gazelles cannot drink salt water like camels do, but they are fast and mobile so that they can go further for fresh water. Also, they feed mainly at night when the leaves of trees and shrubs contain more water than during the day. This is a great help to their water balance. Nevertheless, the larger an animal is, the more it is exposed to heat and drought during the daytime, and the more its internal systems need to become adapted to life in the desert.

The larger mammals of the deserts of the Old World include antelopes, gazelles and wild asses. In the arid regions of North America, there are the Pronghorn (*Antilocapra americana*), formerly very common in the prairies but now extremely rare, and the Mule Deer (*Odocoileus hemionus*). The larger herbivores of the Australian deserts are kangaroos and wallabies. These are marsupials. Their young are born at an early stage of development and are carried

by the mother in a pouch until they are big enough to fend for themselves

None of these animals is able to escape the heat of the day by burrowing, but they do not need much water, and can travel long distances in order to drink. The Dorcas Gazelle (*Gazella dorcas*), one of the smallest of the gazelles with a shoulder height of up to 60 centimetres (2 feet), is widely distributed throughout the Sahara desert. The back and sides are a sandy, reddish-brown and the belly white, the two colours being separated by an indistinct dark stripe. The horns of the male are stouter and more curved than those of the female. In Morocco, Palestine, and other desert regions of the Mediterranean basin, Dorcas Gazelles do not get any water to drink, but can obtain sufficient moisture for their needs from succulent roots and plant material.

Whereas camels are able to survive on a low water intake, the adaptations of Dorcas Gazelles are not so well marked. Their survival depends upon speed and mobility so that they can travel great distances to water. Gazelles can run at up to 80 kilometres (50 miles) per hour. In the Sudan, they migrate to the Nile in the dry season. During the rains herds of two dozen or more can be seen, but in dry weather they are more solitary. In very hot weather, they have been seen to cool themselves in the Red Sea, but they do not drink salt water. A dwarf race of the Arabian Gazelle (*Gazella gazella arabica*), one third of the normal weight, is said to inhabit islands in the Red Sea where no fresh water is available for drinking.

Above:
The Indian Wild Ass (*E. h. khur*) of the Thar desert is able to survive for several days without drinking.

The Saiga (*Saiga tatarica*) is an antelope which roams the arid plains of western Asia, and is about the size of a fallow deer. Its coat is dirty yellowish in summer, longer, thicker and paler in winter. In common with other animals of steppe and desert, where concealment is scarce and sources of water are infrequent, it is speedy and can cover long distances.

Among the most interesting of the hoofed mammals of the African and Asian deserts and steppes are the Wild Asses (*Equus hemionus*). Several subspecies are known, including the Onager (*Equus hemionus onager*) which is the wild ass of the Bible. It is white with a large yellowish area on each flank, and a black dorsal stripe, mane and tail. It lives in herds, each led by an old stallion. The Kiang (*Equus hemionus kiang*) is a deep reddish-brown colour and is more solitary. It inhabits the high desert plateaux of Tibet, Ladak and Sikkim. The Kulan (*Equus hemionus hemionus*) is smaller and sandy-coloured: it extends from the steppes of Transcaspia, Transbaikal and Mongolia into the Gobi desert. African wild asses are represented by the Nubian and Somali races. Probably none of the wild asses of today are pure descendants of the original, true wild ass, and there has been much interbreeding with domestic donkeys.

Asses are sure-footed, long-eared animals that almost rival the camel in their ability to withstand loss of water up to a third of their

body weight. Their drinking capacity is impressive. Within a few minutes they can swallow more than a quarter of their body weight. Asses lose water more rapidly than camels because the fluctuations in their body temperature are smaller. Their coats are thinner and provide less effective insulation.

The Australian Red Kangaroo (*Macropus rufus*) ranges widely throughout the inland desert regions of the continent. These kangaroos can exist on the water content of their herbivorous diet and seldom need to drink. They jump with their hind legs while their bodies are carried well forward and counter-balanced by their massive tails. In this way they can travel for long distances at 30 kilometres (19 miles) per hour. In short bursts a speed of 50 kilometres (31 miles) per hour can be achieved with leaps of over 7 metres (23 feet). Red Kangaroos cool their bodies chiefly by panting. They shelter during the day in rocky outcrops and caves where the humidity is high and if they get too hot, they wet their fur with saliva.

The Australian Quokka (*Setonix brachyurus*) is a smaller marsupial, about the size of a rabbit. It inhabits the offshore islands and coastal regions of south-west Australia where no fresh water is available. It obtains moisture from the vegetation and can drink seawater. In hot weather, as well as losing heat by sweating, the Quokka produces great quantities of saliva, enabling it to lick its feet, tail and belly to make them wet.

Mammals of the cold wastes

The mammals that live in cold places are helped to keep warm by having a small surface-to-volume ratio. The area of their body surface is reduced in relation to their weight. Not only are they larger and heavier than their relations in warmer parts of the world, but their extremities are reduced. For example, the Musk-ox (*Ovibos moschatus*) has very short legs although its body is as heavy as that of a cow. Its neck is thick, its tail small, and its ears are hidden in its furry coat.

Arctic polar mammals can be grouped into a number of categories: carnivores such as bears, wolves, Arctic foxes and weasels which stay throughout the year; larger plant-eaters such as caribou and Musk-oxen which migrate to warmer regions during the winter; and small herbivores, such as lemmings and hares which do not migrate. These cannot hibernate and sleep throughout the winter, as would squirrels and dormice of temperate countries, because the Arctic winter is much too long. So they remain active, foraging under the snow where they are protected from the bitter winds and cold above the ground. They breed rapidly during the brief summer season but cannot reproduce when the temperature is very low.

There are no land mammals in Antarctica. Seals, like penguins, come ashore to breed, but all their food is taken from the sea. Most of the land is covered with a vast ice-cap, which cannot sustain any plant or animal life. When we talk of life in the polar deserts, we are therefore concerned almost entirely with the Arctic.

Like birds, many Arctic mammals have large feet which act as snowshoes. The furry feet of the Polar Bear (*Thalarctos maritimus*) and the spreading hooves of caribou give purchase against firm snow, while the pads of the Arctic Hare (*Lepus arcticus*) are almost twice as big as those of ordinary hares. Of course, the animals of the polar deserts have to keep warm in the coldest weather. Their fur is extremely thick and they are insulated by layers of fat. Even so, many wolves, foxes and weasels are half starved before the long winter is over.

Above:
The Musk-ox, with its short limbs and tail, bulky body and thick hair, shows extreme adaptation to the Arctic climate.

Right:
The Polar Bear of the Arctic has thick fur and its body is insulated by a layer of fat.

Opposite, top:
The Arctic hare, like the Snowshoe Rabbit shown on page 9, has enormous pads to give purchase against the snow and is camouflaged by its white coat.

Opposite, bottom:
Timber wolves feeding on the carcass of a Mule Deer (*Odocoileus hemionus*) that they have killed.

Migration and nomadism

Below:
Varying Hare in winter plumage.

Opposite, top:
Steppe lemmings show regular population cycles in the tundra. When numerous they emigrate in large numbers, but stories of deliberate suicide are mythical.

Opposite bottom:
Population trends of the Lynx and Snowshoe Rabbit in northern Canada showing the dependence of the carnivore upon its herbivorous prey and the long term oscillations in numbers.

By no means all the animals that inhabit deserts reside there throughout all the year. Many of them are migrants which come from afar and only stay for limited periods, during the growing season, when the desert is comparatively benign. Migration is a regular to and fro movement, as a result of which an animal breeds in one part of the world, but spends the remainder of the year somewhere else. Migration may take several different forms, however.

Changing populations

Sometimes, a population becomes very numerous and dense. When this happens, many of the animals leave their homes and emigrate elsewhere. They do not necessar-ily return to the place where they were born, so this is not true migration. In tundra regions especially, lemmings, voles, snowshoe rabbits, and other mammals, show regular cycles in numbers over periods of several years. First, there is a three-year or four-year cycle in the number of lemmings. This is reflected by the snowy owls and Arctic foxes that prey on them. When lemmings are scarce, snowy owls may have to migrate many hundreds of kilometres to the south to find food. Secondly, there is a four-year cycle in the numbers of voles that inhabit the belt of open woodland lying between the tundra and the coniferous forest or 'taiga' to the south of it. Finally snowshoe rabbits and other animals of the

northern forest regions of North America show ten-year population cycles which are reflected in the numbers of their predators, lynxes and wolves.

The reasons for these regular cycles in population numbers are not properly understood. But if, for example, at a particular time, snowshoe rabbits are very numerous, they will eat most of the available vegetation in the area where they are living. When there is little left to eat, many rabbits have to emigrate. Now there are fewer rabbits left, there is less food available for the lynxes and wolves who prey on them, so soon the lynxes and wolves move on. But by this time the vegetation has recovered from overgrazing so the remaining rabbits have plenty of food and few predators, and there are soon a great many rabbits again. The regularity of the cycles may be because the Arctic is a relatively uncomplicated environment, with comparatively few species of plants and animals.

Emigration takes place when population

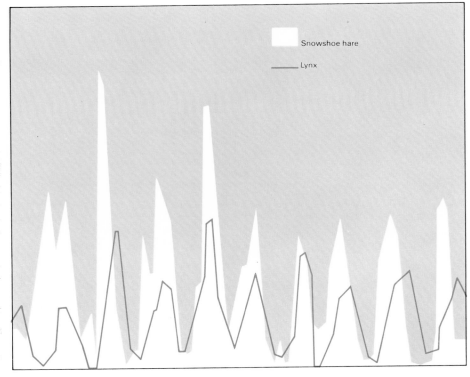

Snowshoe hare

Lynx

numbers reach their peak. It is like steam blowing off through a safety valve! Most probably the majority of emigrants fail to find new homes, and consequently do not survive, but the population, as a whole, benefits. Those animals that do not emigrate are no longer overcrowded and short of food. Instead, they will be healthy parents for the next generation. So, emigration is a very important regulation factor in tundra ecology.

Lemmings – the great trek

The migrations of lemmings only take place when population numbers have increased to such an extent that there is a shortage of food. Many animals are then crowded out from congested areas and take part in spectacular emigrations. As their hordes disperse across the landscape, they are followed by ermine, wolves, Arctic foxes, lynxes, falcons and the snowy owls that feed on them. In Norway the lemmings push irresistibly across the rough mountain sides, and tumble down the slopes, until they reach the sea and plunge in. They have no fear of water and have been known to swim across fiords more than 4 kilometres (2.5 miles) wide. It is not surprising that sometimes they should be swept away by the tides. This has given rise to a legend that they deliberately commit suicide, but that is nonsense. No animal can commit suicide. To do so it would have to understand the meaning of death.

Greenland lemmings migrate over the frozen ocean to the mainland from islands up to 80 kilometres (50 miles) from the shore. When the ice breaks, the little creatures run backwards and forwards looking for a smooth place with a slow current where they may safely cross. Having found one they immediately jump in and swim as fast as they can to the other side. Then they give themselves a good shake, as a dog would, and continue their journey as though nothing had happened.

Circling the globe

Although some birds, such as crossbills and waxwings, show population explosions, and emigrate in large numbers, true migration is more common among the birds of the polar deserts. One of the best-known migrants, the Arctic Tern (*Sterna paradisaea*), breeds in northern Europe and Asia, but migrates as far as Tierra del Fuego and the southern oceans. The Sooty Shearwater (*Puffinus griseus*), which spends the summer in Labrador, Greenland and Iceland, breeds in New Zealand. The tiny Wilson's Storm Petrel (*Oceanites oceanicus*) which is only 18 centimetres (7 inches) long, breeds in Antarctica but enjoys the summer season in the North Atlantic, crossing the ocean in a great loop. Small size is no obstacle to migration, but it would make survival impossible in the polar winter because of an excessive surface-to-volume ratio.

These migrants are sea birds, and fly over the ocean, but swifts, swallows and martins, breed in northern Europe and Asia, and migrate right across the Sahara to spend the winter in southern Africa. It takes all their reserves of food and energy to fly the immense distance across the great desert.

Many other birds from northern Europe and Asia spend the winter on the southern fringe of the Sahara desert. This is the dry season there, during which rain never falls, and the countryside becomes barren and inhospitable. Although insects are scarce and the vegetation is at its least productive at this time of year, these birds manage, nevertheless, to lay down stores of fat in preparation for their northward migration across the desert in the following spring.

Some tropical birds migrate regularly across the equator to stay on the fringes of the desert during the brief rainy season. Abdim's storks breed in July and August, during the rains in the northern savanna and desert regions of Africa. Here they are regarded by local people as 'harbingers of rain'. Then, they move south in October

Right:
The Arctic Tern breeds in northern latitudes migrating to the far South before winter sets in. Few birds undertake more extensive journeys. This one is sitting boldly on a hat.

and November, passing through East Africa during the rainy season there, and inhabit the grasslands of southern Africa during their wet season when it is dry in the north.

Arctic travellers

Most of the Arctic birds migrate in autumn, and only live in the polar desert during the brief summer. This is the time when they lay their eggs. The summer days are endless in the land of the midnight sun, so birds can spend the entire time feeding their chicks on the abundance of insects that appear at this time of year. Resident birds include ptarmigan and the Snowy Owl (*Nyctea scandiaca*), both of which feed on lemmings. Snowy owls are able to catch their prey even in the continuous darkness of the Arctic winter. They have to, since they do not migrate. Although lemmings occasionally do emigrate, followed as already mentioned, by their predators, they never show true migration, but survive the winter in their homes beneath the ice and snow.

The American Golden Plover (*Pluvialis dominica*) migrates from its nesting grounds in the tundra of Alaska and northern Canada to winter in the dry pampas of Argentina, while the Eurasian Golden Plover (*Pluvialis apricaria*) avoids the cold winters by migrating to the deserts of Australia. Migration such as these, often take place not so much to avoid the winter cold as to escape starvation. Neither Musk-oxen, nor the wolves that prey on them, move south in winter. The Arctic Fox (*Alopex lagopus*) even migrates further north at that time, following polar bears, and gnawing the bones of the seals they kill. Both lemmings and snowshoe rabbits remain during the winter and so, of course, does their predator, the snowy owl. The American Black Bear (*Ursus americanus*) only moves southwards during unusually cold winters. Normally it hibernates in Alaska and northern Canada.

Left:
American Golden Plover on its nest. After breeding in the northern tundra these birds migrate to winter in the pampas of Argentina.

In contrast, the Barren Ground Caribou of Canada make extensive migrations in large herds. They inhabit the tundra during the summer, moving southwards through the coniferous forests of the taiga before winter sets in. Caribou follow the same routes year after year and, in places, the rocks have been worn away to a depth of 60 centimetres (2 feet) by the thousands of caribou that have crossed them on countless seasonal migrations. The animals remain in their southern winter quarters until the following spring when they move northwards again. The young are born during the return journey to the tundra, but the caribou do not stop for long. They press onwards, despite all obstacles, and sometimes drown in large numbers as they try to cross flooded rivers.

Below:
Caribou undertake extensive migrations. They are unique among deer in that the females, as well as males, bear antlers.

Right:
Caribou bear their young during the northward spring migration, but this does not delay them for long.

Wanderers of the wastelands
There is never enough food for the larger antelopes of arid regions, such as addax, oryx, gazelles and springbuck, to stay for long in the same place. They have to be constantly on the move, wandering like nomads, from one place to another in search of grass.

In days gone by, the Springbuck (*Antidorcas marsupialis*) of south-east Africa, which is normally nomadic, would occasionally emigrate in incredible num-

bers when the population increased so that there was not enough food for them all. On the larger emigrations, troops of between 10,000 and 20,000 animals would gather together forming columns numbering hundreds of millions. The town of Beaufort West was invaded by a vast number of Springbuck during 1849. These were accompanied by quaggas, wildebeest, eland and other antelopes of all kinds, which filled the streets and gardens as far as could be seen. After three days, the horde disappeared, leaving the countryside looking as though a fire had passed over it!

Another vast column was so large that it took several days to pass by. Many springbuck died, especially old animals and kids, but the survivors headed onwards until they reached the sea. Here they were drowned in such numbers that, for a distance of 50 kilometres (31 miles), the shore was piled high with corpses. The migrating herds were followed by lions, leopards, hunting dogs, jackals, hyenas, and other carnivores that preyed on them.

During their treks, the normal behaviour of the springbuck changed considerably. Like other animals, such as lemmings which migrate in large numbers when food is scarce, migrating springbuck lost their natural shyness. They would enter towns and villages, and even drink from fountains in the street. They were restless, wandered aimlessly about, were startled without cause and would gallop off in any direction until they collected together again.

Nomadic antelopes, like the Addax (*Addax nasomaculatus*), wander across vast areas of desert in search of the ephemeral grasses that spring up after the occasional rain storm. They are able to survive in parts of the Libyan desert where rain is so infrequent that, on average, it only falls once in 10 years at any one place. Indeed, nomadism is the ideal way for larger animals to make the best use of the scarce desert rainfall.

Locusts – plague of the desert

The Desert Locust (*Schistocerca gregaria*), too, is able to exist in the Great Palaearctic desert only as a result of its nomadic habits. Solitary locusts are normally found among sand dunes on coastal plains, in scrub belts along the beds of wadis, in oases and in other similar habitats – islands of green vegetation in the barren desert. The migratory form of the desert locust appears when the population densities build up. Long-distance movements of swarms take place high in the air where wind speeds are often greater than the speed of flight of the locusts. Consequently, it does not much matter in what direction the locusts are actually heading, for they inevitably get carried into areas of low barometric pressure where rain has fallen or is most likely to fall. Here they feed on the ephemeral grasses that spring up and, later, deposit their eggs. The female locust prefers to lay in sand that is dry on the surface but damp underneath, and the eggs do not develop unless they are kept moist.

Other desert insects indulge in nomadic behaviour in order to survive, but none do so quite so dramatically as locusts. The Eighth Plague of Egypt, recorded in the Bible, was a plague of desert locusts, brought by an east wind from Arabia and afterwards cast into the Red Sea by a 'mighty strong west wind'. Locusts of other species are found throughout the deserts of the world, but they are not as destructive as the Desert Locust. The success of these insects in their inhospitable environment, is due entirely to their nomadic habits.

Centre:
The Arabian Oryx is armed with magnificent horns, but Man has exterminated it in its natural home.

Bottom centre:
Wildebeest migrate seasonally to fresh grazing on the great plains of the Serengeti.

Below:
The Desert Locust survives in desert regions only through the nomadic habits that enable it to find the grass that springs up after rain has fallen.

Food chains and interactions

Right:
This hole gouged out by a Gila Woodpecker makes an ideal nesting cavity for this Gilded Flicker.

Below:
The Saguaro is the largest of all North American cactuses, some plants reaching heights of more than 15 metres (50 feet).

The Sonoran desert of Arizona is set in the midst of cowboy country. Unlike the Sahara, or the Gobi desert of Asia in which there are vast regions with little but barren rock and drifting sand, the North American deserts have a surprisingly rich vegetation. Consequently, animal life is relatively abundant. The Giant Saguaro Cactus (*Carnegiea giganteus*) is especially dramatic, with its upraised limbs clothed with pointed spines. These spines not only prevent some animals from feeding on the cactus, but they reflect the sunlight and so help to keep it cool. Drought and heat are the conditions of the desert, but the cacti survive by storing water from one rainstorm to the next. Their fluted stems become so filled with juice that they expand and contract like accordions as the seasons alternate.

Living in the saguaro

The saguaro cactus thrives in the foothills of the mountains but, where the ground levels off, cholla or teddy-bear cacti, prickly pear, paloverde, ocotillo and other plants with melodious Spanish names are more plentiful. Of them all, the saguaro is the most striking, and one part of the Sonoran desert is named after it. This picturesque plant reaches a height of 10-12 metres (33-39 feet) and a diameter of 60-70 centimetres (24-28 inches). Its fruit is eaten by nearly 50 kinds of birds, including thrushes, woodpeckers, pigeons and finches. The Gila Woodpecker (*Centurus uropygialis*) and Gilded Flicker (*Colaptes auratus*) make nesting holes in its trunk. After the young have flown and the holes are deserted, they are used by other kinds of birds such as the tiny Elf Owl (*Micrathene whitneyi*), which is little bigger than a sparrow, screech owls and fly-catchers.

Some of the smaller birds that make use of the saguaro cactus are preyed on by larger predators such as sparrowhawks, but the large Red-tailed Hawk (*Buteo jamaicensis*) feeds mainly on snakes. All animals depend ultimately upon vegetation for their food. The saguaro cactus and other plants provide sustenance for hosts of insects, which are subsequently preyed upon by spiders, lizards and small mammals. These in turn are eaten by larger predators so that what is called a 'food chain' is produced. The 'pyramid of numbers' is perhaps, a more useful concept. According to this, a large volume of vegetation supports many plant-eating animals at the base of the pyramid. These, in turn, are devoured by smaller numbers of predatory

forms. At the top of the pyramid, rests a very small number of the largest predators – such as the puma, or mountain lion, and jaguar.

Many of the smaller animals of the desert shelter from the midday sun in burrows and holes underneath rocks. Some come into the open for short periods to hunt for food. Wolf spiders chase their insect prey. Iguana lizards dash after flies, thereby exposing themselves to attack by even larger predators. Like chameleons, iguanas change colour to match their background, so that

they do not show up too obviously. The regal Horned Lizard (*Phrynosoma cornutum*) is rather slow compared with most lizards. It would easily be caught and eaten if it did not quickly change colour on moving from one place to another. During the heat of the day it buries itself in the sand, and it does so again at night. When it wakes in the morning, it puts its head out into the sunlight. As soon as its brain is warm enough for it to see and think quickly, the Horned Lizard comes right out of the sand and sunbathes until it becomes sufficiently warm all over.

Above:
A food chain in the Great American Desert. Grass is eaten by prairie dogs (E), ground squirrels (F), deer (G), rabbits (H) and kangaroo-rats (I) which in turn, are preyed on respectively by foxes (A), lions (B), lynxes (C) and owls (D).

Above left:
The Red-tailed Hawk makes a ragged nest in the branches of a Saguaro Cactus.

Left:
The Regal Horned Lizard is somewhat slower than other lizards, it therefore needs its ability to camouflage itself for protection.

Above:
A large male tarantula of the Sonoran deserts searching for the burrow of a female, or for the beetles on which it feeds.

Above right:
The Tarantula Hawk Moth feeds on the nectar of flowers, but kills tarantula spiders to feed her young.

Below right:
The Western Diamond-back Rattlesnake (*Crotalus atrox*) is very sensitive to heat and normally hunts after dark when the surface of the desert has cooled.

Below:
The rattle of the rattlesnake is produced by the dry tail segments. These move against each other to produce the characteristic noise.

Then it looks for something tasty for its breakfast. After a midday siesta, buried in the cool sand, the Horned Lizard hunts for another meal before retiring for the night. Tortoises and many smaller desert animals keep to the same sort of timetable.

Others sleep all day and only come out at night, after the sun has set. Many large tarantulas live in the Saguaro desert. At dusk they move to the entrances of their burrows where they wait to pounce on passing insects. Even after sunset, however, they are not safe from enemies themselves. The Tarantula Hawk Wasp (*Pepsis formosa*) is a ferocious wasp which catches tarantulas to feed its larvae. If it can lure a tarantula from its burrow it will paralyse the unfortunate spider with a poisonous sting. Then it digs a hole, drags the tarantula under ground and lays an egg on its body. Other tarantulas are added so that, when the wasp larva hatches, it will have plenty of food ready to feed on.

Unless they are killed by a 'tarantula hawk' or some other enemy, these large spiders will live for many years. The mature males are often to be seen at night on the roads that cross the Saguaro desert, wandering about, looking for the burrows of females. Also to be seen on the roads that cross the Sonoran desert are the Diamond-back Rattlesnake (*Crotalus atrox*) and the Sidewinder Rattlesnake (*Crotalus cerastes*). Of all the desert reptile predators, these are the most efficient and their bite can kill a full-grown man in an hour.

The rattle of a rattlesnake is made of a number of horny pieces of dry skin on the tail. When vibrated rapidly, these produce an angry buzz. This warns other animals to keep away from the rattlesnake, which does not therefore need to waste valuable poison in defending itself. Rattlesnakes feed mainly on mice and kangaroo rats. Between their eyes and nostrils, they have tiny pits, which are sensitive to heat. They therefore

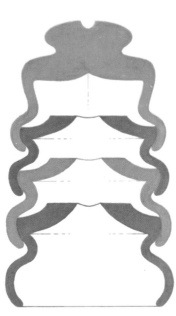

do not need to see, but can strike at warm prey, even in complete darkness, from a distance of 50 centimetres (20 inches) or more.

The victim rarely dies immediately, however, so the snake may need to follow its stricken prey for some distance. Rattlesnakes trail their prey with the help of special sense organs situated inside their mouths. Particles of scent are picked up from the air or ground by the snake's forked tongue and transferred to these wonderfully sensitive organs.

Another reptile of the Sonoran desert is the Gila Monster (*Heloderma suspectum*), one of the only two venomous lizards in the world. It is heavy and clumsy, but because of its poison, the Gila Monster does not need to run away from its enemies. In common with many other potentially harmful animals, it is conspicuously coloured – bright yellow and black. These same warning colours are used by bees and wasps which can inflict a painful sting, and by some caterpillars and beetles which are extremely distasteful.

Of the many fascinating animals that live in the Sonoran desert, it is surprising how many are poisonous. But the desert is a harsh environment. The sparse vegetation provides little cover to hide in, so only the poisonous and speedy, the animals with hard shells (like tortoises), those that can change colour, and those that live in the safety of holes, tend to survive.

Food chains – the links of life

In more extreme deserts such as the Namib and Sahara, vegetation is much less abundant than it is in the northern parts of the Sonoran desert which we have been talking about. Even desert that is completely barren, without any growing vegetation whatsoever, supports a little animal life – a few insects, a scorpion or two, some jerboas perhaps; and a few hawks and snakes that feed on them. It was at one time thought that all these animals must depend, directly or indirectly, on casualties among birds migrating across the desert. Dead birds certainly provide food for scavenging insects and their larvae, which are in turn eaten by scorpions and snakes.

Although jerboas have been found where no other life is apparent, they seem to be limited to within about 50 kilometres (30 miles) down wind of seedling plants. This provides a clue to their source of nourishment. They feed on seeds blown across the desert by the wind.

As to the other animals that live in barren desert, their food too consists of fragments of plant material blown from less infertile places. Much of this is buried, but it does not decay because there are no bacteria in the dry desert sand. Instead, it comes to the surface, often years later, when it provides food for bristletails and the larvae of darkling beetles.

These animals come near the base of the food chains in deserts. They are the herbivores which support the predators and scavengers. Each predator must kill and eat many plant-eaters during the course of its life, and each of these must eat many times its own weight of plant material. In any one food chain, however, there are usually between three and five links. For instance, dried grass may be eaten by beetle larvae,

Above left:
The bizarre shape of this tropical desert web-building spider probably assists its camouflage.

Above:
The Gila Monster advertises its venomous nature by means of its black and yellow colours and, in consequence, is usually left severely alone.

Below:
Examples of food chains in a hot desert. *Left*, grasshoppers (5), beetle larvae (6) and ants (7) are preyed on by camel spiders (1), scorpions (2), ant-lions (4) and jumping spiders (3). *Right*, food chains based on carcasses: a burying beetle (9), fly maggots (8) and a carrion beetle (10).

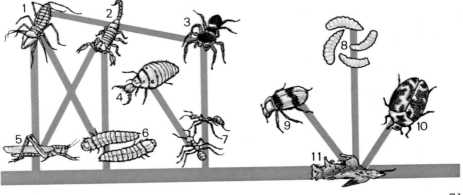

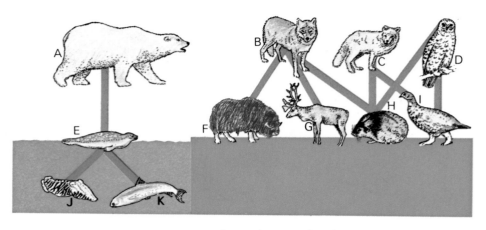

themselves to be devoured by scorpions which, in turn, become food for lizards or birds.

As you go up a food chain, you will find that the size of each predator increases, and the large animals at the top are not preyed on at all. In a three-link food chain in which seeds are eaten by jerboas which are preyed on by hawks, the hawks have no natural enemies at all. They have only disease, starvation and the cruel climate to contend with. Even so, there is a pyramid of numbers, with many small jerboas at the base supporting a few large hawks at the apex. The Chinese proverb, that one hill cannot shelter two tigers, expresses the same idea. Because food is so scarce in arid regions, and competition for it is so intense, we find surprisingly many predators in desert food chains.

The same is true of polar deserts. Microscopic drifting plants in the Antarctic ocean are eaten by tiny animals which form the food of fishes. On these fishes live penguins and seals, whose only enemy is the killer whale. There are no predators on land. Arctic seals are not so lucky. They have enemies on land too – polar bears and Eskimos.

The tundra of the Arctic, in contrast to Antarctica, contains enough plant life to support animal food chains. Lemmings and snowshoe rabbits are preyed on by ermines and snowy owls in one three-unit food chain; lichens are grazed by caribou which are hunted by wolves in another. An extra link is introduced when a small predator, such as an ermine is preyed on by a larger animal such as a wolf.

Because different food chains are linked by other interactions – for instance, if an eagle dies and is eaten by beetles which, in turn, are killed by a snake – it is more accurate to think in terms of food 'webs' rather than of food chains.

Desert camouflage

Desert animals are usually either black or else buff, sandy or reddish-grey in colour. In contrast their undersurfaces are very pale, or even white. This tends to cancel out the effect of the sun's illumination which tends to fall on the back of an animal, leaving its underside in shadow. Thus the animal is helped to merge into its background. Desert is usually open country. There are few trees or boulders large enough to hide any except the smaller animals, so camouflage is important.

In a similar way, most polar mammals and birds are either always white in colour, like the Polar Bear (*Thalarctos maritimus*), or else they become white in winter. In this way both predators and the animals on which they feed become less conspicuous in the snowy landscape. The predators are able to stalk their prey without themselves being seen, but the prey are more difficult to find.

The animals of tropical and subtropical deserts not only harmonize well with the general shades of their backgrounds, but local races are wonderfully adapted to the actual colour of the ground on which they live. The animals that inhabit deserts with black larva soil are usually black, while their relatives, which live on white sand, are white in colour. In deserts where the sand has a reddish shade, the mammals and birds are reddish too. This is readily seen in the case of larks and other ground-nesting birds. Many lizards are even able to change the colours of their bodies so that they match their backgrounds. Some desert butterflies show two seasonal colour forms, so that they can match their background both at the time of the rains and also when the ground is bare of vegetation.

Top:
Examples of food chains in the Arctic desert. *Left*, the Polar bear (A) feeds on seals (E) which, in turn, eat squids (J) and fishes (K). *Right*, the musk ox (F), caribou (G) and lemming (H) are preyed on by wolves (B); while lemmings are also eaten, along with ptarmigan (I) by Arctic foxes (C) and snowy owls (D).

Above:
Mother Cavy (*Microcavia australis*) with her babies in the Patagonian desert of Argentina.

It has been argued that, since rodents and other small mammals are nocturnal and only come out after dark, it cannot benefit them to match their backgrounds. One should, however, remember that the desert air is so clear that nearby objects are visible by starlight even to the human eye and our eyes are not nearly so sensitive at night as those of most predatory mammals. When the moon is full, the scene is bathed with a flood of silvery light so bright that it is possible to read a book or newspaper!

Above:
The Patagonian Gray Fox is more commonly a forest animal but is often found sheltering among the cacti and grasses in desert plains. It hunts mainly by night, resting during the heat of the day.

Left:
The Willow Ptarmigan's feathers provide perfect camouflage against the snowy background of the tundra.

73

Warning coloration

It is quite obvious why it is of advantage to most desert animals to be the same colour as the sand in the area where they live. But why should the remainder be black? Black tends to absorb heat from the sun, which may be an advantage in polar regions, but is a disadvantage in hot deserts.

When the sun's rays are scorching, animals need to be insulated from the heat. Desert darkling beetles, for instance, are usually black. They are also wingless and cannot fly away from the hot sand, but the spaces under their wing cases contain air which insulates their bodies from the heat of their outer surface. They are black because it makes them conspicuous, and this is either an advantage, or at any rate no disadvantage.

Animals may be conspicuous for a number of reasons. It may help them to recognize each other and keep together. It may act as a warning to enemies that they are poisonous or have an unpleasant taste and so are best left severely alone. A common wasp has striking black and yellow stripes which warn us to leave it alone or get stung, so we leave it alone and the wasp does not need to waste its poison. A black desert wasp is even more conspicuous against pale sand than it would be if it were the usual black and yellow colour. Black darkling beetles have a horrible smell and taste, so they are usually left alone too. A scorpion will not eat one until it has been starved for about six months!

Parallel evolution

Because desert conditions are so similar everywhere, desert animals all over the world tend to look very much alike. We have already seen that even though they are not very closely related to one another, small rodents with long back legs used for jumping, are to be found in all tropical and subtropical deserts. Desert hares tend always to have unusually large ears, while many desert mammals, including rodents, bats, hedgehogs, foxes, gazelles, and the Addax (*Addax nasomaculatus*), possess a greatly enlarged bony lump behind their ears. The significance of this enlargement of the skull is not entirely clear, but it probably adds greatly to the sensitivity of the ear, especially to sounds made by enemies such as owls and snakes. It may also aid in the perception of sounds, and vibrations of the ground, made by other heavy animals walking past.

The Sidewinder Rattlesnake (*Crotalus cerastes*) of North American deserts resembles so closely the Horned Viper (*Cerastes cerastes*) of the Great Palaearctic desert that, if one of them did not possess a rattle, it would be very difficult to tell them apart. On top of that, they both move by sidewinding, bury themselves in sand to avoid the sun's heat, and generally behave in much the same kind of way. Similarly, the Saharan Fennec Fox (*Fennecus zerda*) and the American Kit Fox (*Vulpes velox*) look very much alike, but they are not closely related.

Several quite unrelated kinds of desert lizard have adopted a snake-like form of locomotion. The body is covered with smooth scales which cause little friction and the legs may be reduced or even lost, so that movement through the sand is accomplished entirely by wriggling the body. When unrelated animals acquire similar adaptations for a comparable kind of life, we call the phenomenon 'parallel evolution'. Because deserts are remarkably similar to one another, parallel evolution is very common among desert animals. It is seen in their shapes, colours, and behaviour.

Opposite:
The Dama Gazelle (*Gazella dama*) is found from Senegal to the northern Sudan. It is the largest of the gazelles.

Above:
The Whip-scorpion or Vinegaroon is a formidable nocturnal predator, its black colouring warns predators to leave it alone. A warning strengthened by its ability to eject an unpleasant liquid.

Left:
The Persian Horned Viper (*Pseudocerastes cornutus*) is widely distributed throughout the Iranian desert. It looks very like the Sidewinder Rattlesnake of North America.

Above:
Afar nomads travel well armed in the
Danakil desert of Ethiopia.

Man and the desert

The desert has played a very important part in the history and evolution of mankind. As everybody knows, our distant ancestors were quite small, and lived like monkeys in the trees. Here they developed hands with a good strong grip, with the thumb pushing against the fingers, so that they could swing from branch to branch. Their hands continued to be very useful to them when they grew bigger and began to live mainly on the ground, like gorillas do. They could throw things about, and were able to make flint tools and weapons.

The development of large eyes which can focus on the same object simultaneously is another useful adaptation that we owe to our ape-like ancestors. It is essential for accurate distance judging – and you have to

be able to judge distances very accurately if you want to swing or jump from one branch of a tree to another without falling. The eyes of a horse or cow look out on each side of the head with little overlap of vision in front, and these animals cannot judge distances accurately. At some stage of human evolution, our eyes must have got bigger and better, and moved to the front of the skull so that our ancestors were able to judge distances. They also developed colour vision enabling them to recognize flowers and fruit. Apart from monkeys, apes and Men, most mammals are colour blind. Everything looks grey to them.

Humans would never have become as they now are unless our forbears had, at one time, lived in the trees. It seems probable,

76

Above:
Bushmen hunters of the Namib desert
pause to make a fire.

too, that our ancestors must have left the forest and learned to walk on two legs in savanna woodland at the edge of the semi-desert regions of Africa. (Savanna is the name given to the tropical woods and grassland lying between equatorial rain-forest and the deserts to the north and south of it.) At first, the pre-human apes whose descendents were eventually to become Man, fed on roots, berries, fruit, insects, and any carrion they could scavenge. Their upright posture, however, freed their hands for the use of tools and weapons so that they could develop into hunters.

In order to hunt large animals in open savanna country, these ancestors must have learned to cooperate with one another. They also learned to talk, to make fire, and to make flint implements. When they had domesticated the dog, hunting must have become very much easier for them. Today, the Bushmen of the Namib desert and the Australian aborigines still either stalk their prey, or else close in and use spears, clubs, or bows and arrows, while the attention of the quarry is distracted by the hunters' dogs.

During the millions of years during which Man has evolved from his ape-like ancestors, there has been a gradual development in the use of tools and weapons. Eventually, hunting and gathering were replaced by agriculture as a way of life, and finally, when the land became so impoverished that it could no longer support crops, agriculture was succeeded by the herding of animals.

Of every 100 people living in the world, only five inhabit the desert regions. Yet those deserts, hot and polar, occupy well over 30 per cent of the land surface! Because there is so little vegetation, they cannot support very many people. Although hunting and gathering were the original occupations of desert dwellers, today only the Bushmen and Australian aborigines follow this difficult way of life.

Above:
A camp of Bushmen near Tsumkwe in Namibia, resting during the heat of the day.

Primitive people of the deserts

The Bushmen sometimes build huts but do not sleep in them. Each night, they make temporary shelters of branches and grass. They keep no cattle, sheep or goats, but rely for their food on wild animals and plants. The men hunt with spears, clubs and bows. They are magnificent archers and can hit a moving antelope with a poisoned arrow from a distance of up to 150 metres (165 yards). The women and children dig the earth with sticks for edible bulbs and roots which they find with uncanny skill. They collect wild melons and drink their juice. Bushmen obtain water from damp ground, sucking it up through reeds. They store it in empty gourds and ostrich shells. To reduce sweating in hot weather, they urinate in pits dug in the ground, and rest in the damp sand throughout the day. In times of plenty, Bushmen are able to build up reserves of fat in their protuberant buttocks, which gradually waste away during hungry periods. Shy, but intelligent and good natured, they are extremely artistic and have made beautiful rock paintings.

Most of the Australian aborigines have now abandoned their ancient ways of life. Only a few tribes, such as the Bindibu, still roam the deserts of the interior. Here they hunt kangaroos and other game with spears and boomerangs, or gather edible roots and bulbs. These simple people enjoy a complex ritual life which helps them to survive in

extremely primitive conditions. They believe that each clan or tribe is descended from a particular plant or animal which must be protected by magic ceremonies.

The nakedness of the aborigines who, even during cold winter nights, never think of covering themselves, is not due to stupidity or lack of imagination, but to necessity. They have no beasts of burden and cannot afford to weigh themselves down with heavy skin blankets. Instead, they have become adapted to extremes of heat and cold. They are able to sleep naked at night without shivering in frosty weather. Their only shelter is a flimsy windbreak of sticks and grass. Small fires and the bodies of their dogs are their only sources of warmth.

Bushmen do not sleep in their huts but in a circle outdoors, with their feet towards the fire. They cover themselves with skins and are not so well adapted to withstand cold as the aborigines. Even so, their life of hunting and gathering is very primitive compared with that of pastoral herdsmen of other nomadic civilizations.

Human wanderers

By adopting nomadic habits, human beings are able to live permanently in areas where effective rain only falls at intervals of several years. Until recently, the Tibu of the Libyan desert used to wander in small groups, with a few goats, across hundreds

Left:
Despite their harsh existence, Bushmen are good-natured and cheerful. Here some of them are enjoying a dance.

Below:
Arab nomads of the Sahara with the camels on which their lives depend.

Opposite:
Festival among the Tuarego at Djanet in Algeria.

Right:
The flowing garments of the Arabs provide shelter from the sun and wind.

Below:
Women of the Firouzkuhi tribe with their gaily coloured tents, near Chakcharan, Afghanistan.

to the cool deserts and steppes of Central Asia, where Bactrian camels replace the dromedary. In earlier times, the Huns, Mongols, and other nomadic tribes of Central Asia developed the art of riding and fighting on horseback with lance or bow so effectively that, by the 13th Century, they had become invincible.

Some pastoral nomads are always on the move, following in the wake of scattered desert rainstorms so that there will be grass for their camels and goats. Others are nomadic only during the rains, and spend the dry season in villages clustered round wells and on the banks of rivers. They can never stray too far from water, except when the vegetation is exceptionally luxurious. Then their camels do not need to drink at all, and the nomads subsist on camels' milk. Sheep and goats, however, cannot survive without drinking at least once every three or four days, so they are unable to graze too far from wells and waterholes.

The nomadic way of life is hard, but nomads are fiercely proud and independent people. They consider themselves far superior to people who live in houses, but they need to trade with them. In exchange for milk, meat, hides and wool, the nomad receives dates, grain, salt and other necessities of life. By making use of horses, camels, donkeys, burros, yaks and llamas, the nomads of the world's deserts are able to exist without permanent homes. The Bedouin live in black tents of woven goat hair, stretched over light-weight poles. These tents provide shade, and shelter from the wind and sand. They can easily be carried on the backs of camels. The nomads of the Gobi desert ride horses to herd their yaks, and live in portable tents of felt, stretched over collapsible frames of willow branches.

The nomadic herdsmen of the Great Palaearctic desert would not dream of travelling almost naked, like Bushmen or aborigines. They wrap themselves up in voluminous clothing to provide shelter from the sun and wind. The Tuareg of the Hoggar mountains, who are of Berber stock, even veil their faces with the dark blue cloths that make these people so colourful. At one time they, with other nomadic tribes, controlled all the camel caravan trade of the Sahara, and acquired a tremendous reputation as bandits.

Before Algeria was settled, Berbers and Arabs were great raiders, and operated over a vast area of desert. The Chaamba Arabs, however, experts in desert warfare, were only too pleased to join the French camel corps and fight their traditional enemies, the Berbers. They became excellent soldiers and it was one of their patrols that broke for ever the military power of the Tuareg at the Battle of Tit on 7 May, 1902.

During the peaceful years of the present century, the numbers of pastoral nomads

of kilometres of almost lifeless country where it rains, on average, only once every 30 to 50 years — except in a few isolated areas of high ground where the figure is reduced to a storm once every four to 10 years.

Nomadic tribes of herdsmen are found all over the Great Palaearctic desert. Some tribes are small, with little social organization, while others are divided into large clans with elaborate social, political and economic systems. They move within allotted territories which are often marked by wells and springs.

The nomadic tribes of the Sahara and of the deserts of western Asia travel on dromedaries, driving their herds of sheep and goats with them. They value horses greatly, but these animals are better suited

have increased greatly. So, also, have the populations of oasis dwellers – which is why the desert has expanded so rapidly. Too many people living in the same place results in their domestic animals over-grazing the land. In addition, trees are cut down for firewood and the land becomes infertile through over-cultivation.

Settled life is only possible in irrigated areas and oases. The earliest civilization of Asia and Africa depended on the irrigation of fertile land along the valleys of great rivers such as the Tigris, Euphrates, Indus, Hwang-ho and Nile. In South America early civilizations also depended on irrigation from the shorter rivers crossing the Atacama desert.

The Pueblo Indians made an art of building thick-walled mud or 'adobe' houses, roofed over with clay-covered poles. In Africa and parts of Asia, oasis dwellers also build their houses of thick mud. These houses are very cool and airy but, in heavy thunderstorms, they disintegrate and collapse. In some places, near swamps and marshes where reeds are available, these too are used for building. The marsh Arabs of Iraq and the people who live near Lake Chad usually live in houses built of reeds or papyrus.

The oases of Asia and Africa have long

Below:
Amerindian cutting wood for the oven at Taos Pueblo in New Mexico.

Bottom:
A palm grove in the oasis of El Oued, Algeria. Encroaching sand is a constant threat to desert oases.

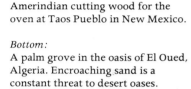

and important histories. They have been so completely changed by human activities that we do not know what their original vegetation was like. In the Sahara and the Arabian desert, the most important oasis crop is the date palm, in whose shade grow lemons, limes and fruits and vegetables. These are often of high quality and with aromatic flavour or scents. They include olives, figs, apricots, guavas, pomegranates, wheat, maize, millet, lucerne, peas, beans, onions, pimentos, sweet potatoes and tobacco. The date palm provides fruit for eating and for distilling alcholic drinks. The stones are ground up to feed camels, the leaves are used as fuel for cooking, and their fibres are twisted into ropes, or woven into a coarse cloth. This is used to cover the wooden frames in which agricultural produce is carried about. Finally, the trunks of dead palms are used for building houses, so absolutely nothing is wasted!

Left:
Sheep leaving a water hole in the Danakil desert. Domesticated animals are more dependent than wild game on drinking water.

Above right:
Eskimo seal hunter paddling through thin ice at a floe edge on his way to collect a seal he has shot.

Below right:
A Polar Bear scavenging from a garbage dump at Churchill, Manitoba. Wild animals often adapt themselves to the presence of Man.

Dwellers in the far north

So far we have been talking only about the people who live in hot deserts. The Eskimos of the northern polar regions are also desert dwellers, so are the nomadic Lapps and Samoyeds. But the bitter cold of the winter is so great that only a few groups of Eskimos inhabit the Arctic permanently, and the Antarctic has no indigenous peoples at all.

Eskimos depend for food largely upon the animals of the sea. They will stay, sometimes for days, beside a hole in the ice, waiting for a seal or sealion to surface for breath. Then they spear the unfortunate animal and drag it ashore. The oil from its fat or blubber provides them with light and heat, and they gorge themselves on the raw meat until they can eat no more. Their herds

Below:
A bull Caribou, which has been shot, outside the cabin of Eskimo fur trappers in the North-western Territories of Canada.

Above:
Eskimos starting to build an igloo, cutting the blocks out from a trench, in the North-western Territories of Canada.

Right:
Eskimo fur trapper setting a marten trap.

of reindeer also provide them with food and clothing. In Greenland Musk-oxen are hunted for these purposes.

Eskimos build their homes of stones, peat, driftwood, bones and skin. Igloos, made of blocks of snow, with a sheet of ice for a window, are used only for temporary camps by people travelling in winter. Although made of freezing snow, these igloos become so warm and fuggy inside that the inhabitants take off their fur clothes.

The harsh conditions of their life tend to make Eskimos staunch individualists. They use dogs to pull their sledges and show great skill in constructing kayaks or skin-covered canoes. In olden days, their clothes were made entirely of the skins of seals, reindeer, polar bears, dogs or Arctic foxes, sewn together with threads made from animal sinews. Now, of course, they wear clothes made of wool and cloth. Formerly, when two people met, they would greet one another by rubbing noses together, but this practice has long been abandoned.

Technology comes to the deserts

Since oil and minerals have been discovered in Alaska, there has been a great influx of people and machinery into the Arctic. Eskimo hunters and trappers now use snowmobiles and rifles, so that much of the wildlife is becoming endangered. The vegetation, too, is suffering from overgrazing by Musk-oxen and reindeer, and is being harmed by vehicles and ski trails. The tundra is vulnerable to over-exploitation and, like the vegetation of tropical and subtropical arid regions, it is easily destroyed by misuse.

The men and machines that have appeared from the more complex world to the south have greatly affected the lives of the Eskimos. With improved medical facilities and hygiene, their numbers have increased, as have their material desires. The economic development of the Arctic regions, with the help of western technology, will undoubtedly leave scars, not only on the land but also on its people.

The same thing has taken place in the tropical and subtropical regions of the world, especially where oil is being exploited. Here the life of the local people has changed beyond recognition. Nowadays, as well as camels, you can see expensive motor cars drawn up outside the tents of the Bedouin in Saudi Arabia and Kuwait. Camel caravans are becoming a thing of the past. In their place, goods are taken across the Sahara by lorry.

Instead of becoming adapted to the hostile climate, Europeans often use technology to change the microclimates in which they live. Electric fans, evaporative coolers, air conditioners and heat transfer systems are used to cool or warm the insides of houses. Fresh food is flown in from abroad and the foreigners isolate themselves as much as they can from the environment around them.

I think this is a great mistake. Modern houses are often hotter than traditional mud-walled buildings. If you do live in a modern house, it is better to make do with a large sweep fan than to indulge in expensive air conditioning, because, every time you go out, it seems hot and uncomfortable. The more one gets accustomed to, and forgets the heat and discomfort of the desert climate, the less it impinges on every day life. In order to adjust to desert conditions one has to change one's way of life to some extent. But how else can one understand and get to know the real people of the desert?

Below:
A lorry stirs up clouds of dust in the Sahara desert near Tegguidda, in Niger.

The world's enlarging deserts

During the last hundred years or so, the deserts of the world have been expanding at an alarming rate. The Sahel savanna regions on the southern borders of the Sahara, much of Somalia, and the fringes of the Thar desert of India and Pakistan, for instance, are now dry and barren, yet within living memory they were green and fertile. This has not happened only because of a shortage of rain. They have been turned into desert by the unwitting mistakes of human beings.

Desertification

Some deserts are naturally barren. Parts of the Atacama of Peru and Chile are almost without vegetation because the rainfall is so low – only one year in 10, on average, has more than 2 millimetres (0.01 inches). But many deserts have quite enough rain to support rich vegetation if they are left to themselves. Many regions which now are barren have much the same amount of rain as they did when they were green and fertile. It is when such land is misused by its human inhabitants that it turns into a desert. When the plants have been eaten by sheep, goats and cattle, these areas become as barren as the Atacama. The fortified Mogul city of Jaisalmer, in Rajesthan, was once an affluent trading centre on a caravan route. Now it is little more than a beautiful museum in the desert sands of the Thar.

It is not only overgrazing that makes these arid regions so barren. When the soil is trampled and compressed by the countless hooves of domestic stock, such rain as falls is prevented from sinking in. Even dead plants help rainwater to penetrate into the soil, but if there is no vegetation at all to prevent it from running away, the water pours down the desert wadis in roaring torrents, causing erosion and washing all the topsoil away as it does so. At one time the presence of too many cattle produced desert-like conditions in the northern Ugandan province of Karamoja, where the annual rainfall can be as high as 64 centimetres (25 inches) a year. However the vegetation soon re-established itself when tsetse flies invaded the land. The people moved elsewhere, taking their stock with them because tsetse flies infect cattle with a fatal disease known as 'nagana'.

The presence of trees and grasses not only prevents soil erosion from taking place, but causes less moisture to be lost through evaporation, since the ground is shaded from the fiery blast of the tropical sun. Unfortunately once the grass has been

Opposite:
Sheep grazing in Morocco with the snow-covered Jebel Ayachi in the background.

89

eaten by sheep and goats, and the trees have been cut down for fuel, it is difficult for the vegetation to become re-established in places where there is little rainfall. In addition, as the soil is blown away in fine dust, it causes the atmosphere to become heated at higher levels. This prevents the formation of rain-bearing clouds so, eventually, rainfall itself is reduced.

Another cause of desertification is cultivation of the soil in marginal areas of savanna at the desert's edge. When drought follows a few years of good rainfall, cultivated soil that has been broken up in agriculture is readily blown away as fine dust. When small areas are farmed traditionally with hoes or ox ploughs, little harm is done to the environment, but mechanized agriculture and the use of tractors cannot fail to cause rapid soil erosion.

Desert land reclaimed

One way of overcoming these problems, and of making the desert blossom, is to obtain water for irrigation. However, this raises further problems. Much of the water underlying the Sahara, for instance, is mineralized, and cannot be used by plants or drunk by animals. Desalinization is costly, and requires skilled labour which is often not available. In many deserts, subterranean water is a fossil resource. It has been stored underground for thousands of years and is not being replenished. When it is pumped up, the level of the water-table drops steadily. This is probably the case in many parts of the Sahara, including much of Algeria and Libya. So, although many crops per year can be grown in the brilliant desert sunshine, the wells will soon run dry. In Lower California, short-term farming projects are based on wells which are expected to last for no more than 15 years at the most.

Desert soils are often naturally fertile because there has been little or no rain to wash away the nutrients that growing plants require. Unfortunately, the addition of irrigation water often results in dissolved salts being drawn upwards through the soil, as a result of evaporation at its surface, and here they are deposited as an infertile crust. Salinization has plagued most areas of irrigation agriculture and is very difficult to overcome. The simplest way to remove unwanted salts is to wash them away with large amounts of fresh water, but this can only be done if there is good drainage. Irrigated fields have to be levelled for the distribution of water, and this makes for poor drainage.

About one third of the Indus valley irrigation system has been affected by waterlogging, and even more suffers from salinity. Despite several costly projects intended to reverse these trends, productive land is still being lost to agriculture. The same is taking place in China, Israel, Iraq, Syria, Mexico, Brazil, Patagonia, Argentina and other parts of the world where irrigation schemes have been introduced.

Below:
Orchard of fruit trees in the Jordan Valley. Where there is water for irrigation the desert can be extremely fertile.

Perhaps the greatest disadvantage of
large-scale irrigation schemes in desert
regions is the increase in human diseases
which accompanies them. Of these, bilhar-
zia, onchocerciasis and malaria are undoubtedly the most important, but there
are many others. At the same time, desert
irrigation schemes may provide permanent
breeding places for locusts and other
agricultural pests. At one time people
thought that, if water were provided, all
would be well. At last some authorities are
beginning to realise that the situation of the
desert is more complicated than this!

It is very easy to degrade arid and semi-
arid environments into desert, but it is
difficult and costly to reverse the process.
By adding to the number of places at which
livestock can secure water, the area of
grazing can be widened, which helps to
reduce the pressure around the original
sources of water. This can be achieved by
boring new wells and by constructing arti-
ficial ponds to trap the seasonal rainfall.
Such methods are effective, however, only
so long as the herds are not permitted to
increase in numbers. If they do increase, the
situation becomes worse, not better. This is
what recently happened on the Sahel savanna region of Africa. By 1970, the land was
supporting 24 million people and about
the same number of cattle. This was roughly
a third more people and twice as many

animals as in 1930. The effect of providing
more wells had been simply to make past-
ure, instead of water, the limiting factor.
Consequently, when the inevitable period
of drought came, its effect was all the more
devastating. Thousands of dying cows clustered around the wells. Indescribably
emaciated and with bloated bellies, they
would stagger away from the churned mud
at the water's edge to search for food. Each
well and bore-hole quickly became the
centre of its own little desert about 40-50
kilometres (25-30 miles) square!

The nomadic way of life

Although the herding of sheep, goats and
cattle is a major cause of desert expansion,
pastoral nomadism is a remarkably efficient
adaptation to the uncertainties of the desert
climate. The movements of the nomads are
not random. In the Sahara, for instance,
they move as far south during the dry
seasons as they can go without entering the
range of tsetse flies. With the first rains,
however, the grass springs up and the herds
begin to move northwards until the edge of
the desert is reached. Then the southward
journey begins again. This time, the cattle
graze the grass that has grown up behind
them on their northward journey, and
drink the standing water that remains from
the rainy season. In their dry season area,
they find a crop of grass and stubble that

Above:
This view of the Namib gives an idea of the beauty and solitude to be found in the desert.

will have to last them for eight or nine months, until the rains come again. In desert regions where the climate is even more extreme than in the Sahelian zone of Africa, nomadism is the only way of life by which Man can survive, except in oases.

Although the nomadic way of life is probably the only one which will ever produce much in the way of food from arid desert regions, government policies towards nomadism are usually unimaginative and unenlightened. They appear to be directed chiefly towards settlement of the nomads and restriction of their migration routes. If traditional nomadism were to disappear, however, vast areas of desert that produce some food would become permanently useless to mankind. It would be better to encourage and modernize the nomads' way of life. The hardships and shortages these people have to endure could be alleviated by a flying-doctor service, mobile markets and schools. Grazing could be controlled and even improved. News of distant rainfall could be transmitted by

radio, and so on. In this way, the deserts of the world might continue to contribute usefully to the economy of man, provided of course, that they were not over-exploited.

Bringing the deserts into the modern world

Another way in which desert and semi-desert could be developed in the service of mankind, without further destruction of the habitat, is by game ranching. Wild game are so much more mobile than domesticated animals that they do not normally cause overgrazing or soil erosion. Futhermore, they require less water, partly because they feed mainly at night when leaves contain more water than during the day. Oryx and Addax antelope, for instance, inhabit desert where there is *absolutely* no water for them to drink. Instead of protecting these wonderful animals so that they could provide a constant source of meat and hides, Man has almost exterminated them! This is just about as stupid as killing all the whales!

A certain amount of semi-desert country can be farmed by water that runs off from rainstorms, provided the land is left fallow for some 15 or 20 years before it is cropped again. Millet and sorghum grown in this way, can provide food without harming the land. When crops like groundnuts are introduced to earn foreign currency, however, fertility declines. This is because desert regions cannot take the strain of intensive agriculture.

Economy of water is vital for efficient agriculture in desert regions. The traditional agricultural methods of oasis dwellers, which have developed over a long period of time, are very economical. Even more efficient use of the existing water can, however, be made by hydroponic cultivation. Nutrient solutions pumped once or twice daily through plastic pipes perforated by small holes, irrigate the roots of plants growing in the sand. The surface of the soil is not wetted, so little water is wasted through evaporation. In this way, the amount of water required to grow tomatoes, for example, may be reduced by more than half.

There are other ways in which modern technology can be used to develop the desert for the benefit of mankind without causing serious harm to the environment. Sand dunes can be stabilized and sown with grasses, or planted with trees. The procedure is complicated and expensive, however, and requires large numbers of men and machines.

The most sought-after riches of the world's deserts are the deposits of oil and minerals that lie underground. In addition, however, tropical deserts possess an inexhaustible supply of solar energy. This can already be harnessed for research and domestic purposes and could, one day perhaps, provide power for industry. A manufacturing economy uses less water per head of population than does agriculture. A day may even come when enlightened industry expands in desert countries of the world, while the industrial countries of today concentrate more on the agriculture for which their climates are better suited. The problems of arid lands are complex and have no single solution. The more ways in which a region can be rationally exploited at the same time, however, the less the environment will be harmed.

Desert expansion is one of many consequences of the world's current population explosion and it is no use attempting to deal with it in isolation. It is taking place at a

Above:
Hydroponic farming in USA. These ornamental plants are being grown on solutions of nutrient chemicals, with very little water required.

Left:
A herd of Addax. These antelope can survive in waterless desert: if protected they could be a perpetual source of meat and hides.

Right:
Tomatoes can be grown in winter in Tunisia as a cash crop for export to snow-bound Europe.

Below:
This pipeline at Rosh Pina, Higher Galilee, serves the area with water from the North.

time when more than half the people in the world are suffering from malnutrition. There is a striking relationship between the poverty of a region and its tendency to become desert. As people are driven from their homes, they settle on the edge of the desert they have made, and begin the process all over again. Yet, what else can they do? They have to eat, and their goats and sheep are all that they have.

Nor is the problem confined to tropical and subtropical deserts alone. As we saw in the last chapter, the tundra and polar deserts are also under threat. Throughout the centuries, man has consistently been reducing the productive capacity of arid lands by over-exploiting their resources. The time has come when we must be prepared to invest some of our profits in the lands from which they have been gathered. The fight against the desert must be fought not merely to save human life and reduce suffering. It must be fought to improve the quality of life for future generations. Until the western world devises an economy in which affluence is not based on waste, pollution and exploitation, it cannot expect other, less fortunate cultures not to do the same.

In the rat-race of modern society, we often get tired of crowded cities, and long for the wide open spaces – for the desert wastelands. Air transport places the world at our doorstep. One day the tourist value of the deserts may come to exceed the value of their mineral wealth. When that time comes, the efforts of scientists and conservationists to preserve the desert countryside, with its extraordinary variety of plants and animals, will have been worthwhile.

Index

In this Index D. represents Desert. Textual reference is in Roman and captions to illustrations in Italic.